DAD
SKILLS

How to

BE AN AWESOME FATHER & IMPRESS ALL THE OTHER PARENTS

CHRIS PETERSON
AUTHOR OF *MANSKILLS*

COOL
SPRINGS
PRESS

Brimming with creative inspiration, how-to projects, and useful information to enrich your everyday life, Quarto Knows is a favorite destination for those pursuing their interests and passions. Visit our site and dig deeper with our books into your area of interest: Quarto Creates, Quarto Cooks, Quarto Homes, Quarto Lives, Quarto Drives, Quarto Explores, Quarto Gifts, or Quarto Kids.

24 23 22 21 20   1 2 3 4 5

ISBN: 978-0-7603-6754-4

Digital edition published in 2020

Library of Congress Cataloging-in-Publication Data available

Design: Landers Miller Design, LLC

Page Layout: John Hall Design Group

Illustration: Jon Cannell

Printed in Canada

Contents

Introduction

Ah, the good old days. Back in the day, it was a given that "Father Knows Best." Children never questioned the man of the house. He was expected to go to work during work hours, bring home the bacon, and fix the car when it broke down. The kids? Well, let's just say it was a hands-off parenting generation.

Of course, back then, most dads also believed the garnish on the steak was the closest you should get to vegetables on a plate, that a nightly cocktail or four was the proper way to unwind, and that real men ate a daily dose of blood-red meat and accepted the inevitably fatal heart attack in their fifties. A lot has changed since those times, but one thing remains true: Father is still expected to know best. And that right there is what this book aims to ensure.

It's a tall order. Kids are handful and half at any given moment in history, but modern times have thrown a mess of technology and an increasingly complex world into the parenting mix. Become a parent and you were always going to have to deal with a generous mix of hormones, temper tantrums, ungodly messes, and busy school schedules. But nowadays? Get ready to be the much-maligned screen-time cop, coordinator, and chauffeur for all things social and watcher for the subtle signs that your kiddie is being bullied. Holy heck, dadding could be a full-time job these days.

But not for a Dadskills man. You're the type of guy who has mastered opening a beer without an opener. You know how to drift a car like a stuntman and generally make your way through the world like a boss. Dad-dom? Oh, you so got this, Jack.

That's, in part, thanks to the handy 411 in the chapters that follow, covering the full spectrum of fathering. You'll find every little need-to-know strategy and tip, from welcoming your new bundle of joy in the delivery room all the way to joyfully bundling your burden off to college and out of the house. You'll find soup-to-nuts coverage to avoid a dreaded social services visit, and for your part, you just need to bring two things to the party: the ability to keep a cool head (repeat after us: you are smarter than a four-year-old) and your well-developed sense of humor. That last one comes in particularly handy the first time Little Miss Attitude tells you she hates you, before storming off and slamming the door to her room. Remember that you were her hero once, and you will be again.

1

You're freaked out
and chances are
you might be
scared witless.

CHAPTER 1

Baby Wrangling

Eagerly expecting your first rug rat? Experiencing the joy of being a first-time parent? Indulging the pure bliss of caring for your tiny, tiny bundle of love? No, you aren't. You're freaked out and chances are you might be scared witless. Well, don't be. First of all, you'll be fine. Second, for Pete's sake, you're a Dadskills man. Dadskills men don't do scared witless.

Now look, you're going to have a lot of people tell you, "Well, there's no manual for raising children." Our answer? Since when you did *you* ever need a manual? Not when you rebuilt that 1967 Charger from the wheels up. Not when you renovated your dark basement into a deluxe home theater. And you won't need it now, on your way to raising a healthy, happy, smart, and successful person.

When other parents fret if the bottle's going to ruin their kid and debate whether it's "raising" or "rearing," you're getting on with the job of being a fabulous new parent, enjoying every minute, and making that little baby as happy as a clam. Start with the fact that you are not alone—far from it. You'll have a helper every step along the way as you shepherd your bumble from infancy onward, in the easy-to-use form of the rock-solid advice in this chapter.

That great kid adventure begins in the run-up to the actual birth. A little heads-up on what's to come can only make you and your better half calmer in the madness that is a delivery room. You'll find here a breakdown on all the essentials so that you can feel a little more like "I'm witnessing a miracle" and a little less like "What the hell is happening?"

Then it's on to the nitty and the gritty of keeping the child happy and healthy— more gritty than nitty if we're being honest here. Skip through this chapter and you'll find essential advice on the best ways to handle all those diapers your little poop factory will produce and to keep the apple of your eye clean and healthy from stem to stern. Ultimately, though, the best info is all about how to make your life a little easier by making your bumble's life a little easier.

Mom's job is to get that baby out of her. Getting the "go bag" ready for the grand event is yours. Have it all ready by the thirty-fifth week and stock it with general essentials for a possible multinight stay, and whatever particulars will make the event more comfortable for both of you.

Must-haves: Copy of your insurance card; toiletries bag, with everything both of you might need; change of clothes for both of you; backup phone charger(s) if you have them; extra pair of glasses if you wear them; eye mask and earplugs or noise-cancelling headphones (can also be good for soothing music or soothing silence); warm, nonskid socks; maternity bras and maternity pads; high-energy snacks; and bottled water.

Specific needs: Her favorite bathrobe, slippers, and pillow (all cleaned before you pack them); a music player if you use one, with a birthing playlist if she wants music; your individual birth plan if you have one; some sort of soft hair tie; good book in case of long labor; camera (or smartphone) if you *both* want pictures; massage oil if she's hip to being massaged.

SURVIVE A WIFE IN LABOR

It's a time-tested rule: When mama bear is happy, everyone is happy. Trust this as gospel. Keep your mama bear comfortable during the process of becoming a mama bear and you will realize the benefits tenfold down the line. The first commandment for dads during labor is, *Keep a cool head and be seen more than heard.* Communicate for her only when she wants you to, and keep your jokes and chatter to a minimum. Minimum means zero.

Remember, first and foremost, this ain't about you. Take nothing personally. Be involved only if and when she wants you to be involved. Do not give unsolicited back rubs unless you want to see fangs. You don't want to see fangs, do you? Do not, do not, do not freak out no matter what you see or hear. Be her lackey. Whatever she wants, however demanding, supply it. And most of all, be there for every moment—not worrying about what's happening at work or anywhere else in the world.

SET UP A CRIB PROPERLY

Setting up a crib in these modern times is a matter of "simpler is better." Keep in mind that the whole exercise is about preventing the horrifying and somewhat mysterious Sudden Infant Death Syndrome (SIDS). Babies really use the crib only for sleeping, so safety is the number-one concern.

Gone are the days when a crib resembled a miniaturized version of a five-year-old's bed. Start with the crib itself; it should be new. This is one nursery addition that you should never buy secondhand, because modern crib design is radically different from models of even a few years ago. For instance, drop-down sides were once all the rage; they are now considered unsafe and dangerous.

As much as you are a guy who operates outside the boundaries of manuals and installation instructions (props, man), this is one case where you need to follow those dreaded manufacturer's instructions to the letter. Crib makers put those instructions together as protection against liability, so the instructions are very well thought out and safety oriented. Follow them.

Be sure to check that nowhere on the sides is there a gap large enough for a baby's head to slip through—especially important if you're the new papa of a preemie or just a particularly small infant. If there is mesh netting around the outside of the crib, check that the openings in the netting are not large enough for the baby or any clothing to get caught in it.

The mattress should fit snug; it should be hard to get your fingers down between the crib side and the mattress. Likewise, the mattress sheet should be a tight fit, specifically meant for that mattress. And guess what? You don't need anything else in there besides the baby. No bumpers, no pillows, no stuffed penguins, or toys. Just kiddo and the crib. Full stop. Follow the most current recommendations and lay the little one on his or her back when it comes time for a snooze. Then hope and pray for a solid four hours during which you can explore your own sleep chamber.

CATCH THE BABY

Well, you wanted to show her what a great partner you are. So now you'll get as up close and personal as it gets—to "catch" that baby. The professional is going to be the one to guide that newborn out of the path all newborns must take. You'll be laying on hands just as the baby is completely "out." The wonderful thing here is that you will be the first human skin in contact with that child (other than the mother), because the birthing professional will be wearing gloves. Which is why it's crucial that you wash those paws thoroughly.

Make your intentions clear to the doctor, nurse, or midwife who will be guiding the little bundle into your hands. Be sure handed and realize that newborns are messy and slippery. The pro on hand will instruct where to put your hands and will stick close to ensure the child is secure. That person will help you move the baby to the mother to wait for the cutting of the cord. And pal, man up if you're the queasy sort. You don't need to be adding to the chaos by vomiting or passing out.

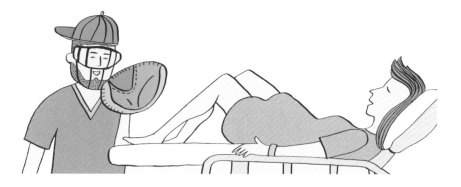

DEAL WITH UNWANTED ADVICE

Want to find out how many baby experts you have in your life? Just wait till you bring your newborn home. Then everyone and his barber is Dr. Spock. You could ignore it all, but it's important to remember: Many of these buttinskies are potential future babysitters. Much as you may not want to be, be diplomatic.

A grain of salt is important. Even the most well-intentioned advice (looking at you, Grandma and Grandpa) may be years, if not decades, out of date. That said, always be a little open to unique parenting insight—as long as it comes from an actual parent.

Be the bigger person in all cases. You're only stockpiling good mojo when you make nice sounds that suggest you're grateful for the advice. A simple thanks is a feel-good reply that sounds like your accepting the advice even if you're laughing inside. If the advice giver is also a long-winded droner, don't hesitate to use your baby as an excuse—you have to get home for the baby's nap or feeding.

TIME CONTRACTIONS

You didn't have to cart a big round body around for nine months. You didn't have deal with boundary-defying people feeling free to touch your ever-growing stomach. So the least you can do is handle the math once labor starts. That means timing contractions.

If she's fighting the pain of contractions, chances are she can't communicate when they start and end. You'll have to be in tune with her to figure that out. A stopwatch is handy because your phone may not be. Time the duration of each contraction and the period between the end of one and the start of another. Make two columns on a piece of paper and enter the time between one contraction and the next, and how long each lasts. The general rule of thumb is "the 411 rule": Call the expert when there are four minutes between contractions that last for one minute, and the contractions have been steady for more than one hour. Defer to your doctor's or midwife's recommendations before heading to the hospital or sending out a distress signal.

INSTALL A CAR SEAT CORRECTLY

The National Highway Traffic Safety Administration estimates that three out of four infant car seats are installed incorrectly. Don't be a part of that club. Start with the car. The car seat will be installed in the back seat and, ideally, the center position. Some cars don't accommodate center mounting. Know your car and check your owner's manual before installing the car seat. Never use a secondhand car seat, because it might be too far out of date and not in keeping with current safety recommendations.

Place the base first. Position it and adjust the angle, checking the integral angle indicator is at 35 to 45 degrees. If there is no angle adjustment on your model, use a firm bolster underneath and a bubble level on the armrest of the seat to get it to the correct angle. Next secure the base with a seatbelt run through the base's belt channels. Secure the belt with the base's tightener or according to the manufacturer's instructions. The base should move less than 1 inch (2.5 cm) side to side.

If your car is newer than 2002, it has a Lower Anchor and Tethers for Children (LATCH) system, concealed behind discreet buttons on the seats. Attach the base anchors to the seat and tighten with the base's LATCH-adjustment strap. Check the forward-and-back and side-to-side movement of the seat again.

Now it's time to put that car seat in place. Secure it in the base. (If it's a rear-facing-only model, make sure it's facing the back of the car. Otherwise you want it facing forward so that you can easily keep tabs on the baby.) Last, but not least, secure your bundle of love in the seat with the baby's back flat against the bed of the seat and snug the restraining straps over the shoulders. Give the restraints the "pinch test"; if you can pinch the belt into a fold, it's not tight enough. Pull the strap to tighten it further. Congratulations, Dad—you're ready to roll!

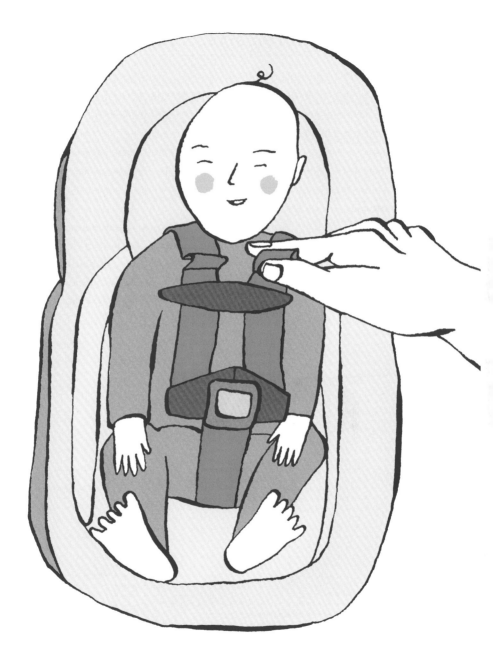

HELP HER PUSH

It's cruel irony that right when a birthing woman most needs to exert herself in the final push to birth, she's at the tail end of a body-draining marathon that may have lasted days. Low on energy, fuel, and patience, the last thing your wife wants to do is push. Don't stand idly by; you can help.

Depending on where you are (birthing center, hospital, home, the back of a taxi) and the medical pro (doctor, midwife), your wife may be urged to push as soon as she dilates, or as she feels ready and only in response to the urge to push (called "spontaneous" pushing).

If she's on a hospital bed, the best you will be able to do is stand alongside her and hold her back and one leg to provide resistance (a nurse will do the same on the opposite side). If you're in a birthing center or at home, you may be able to get in the luge position, seated behind the mama to be. Reach around and grab her thighs and lean your chest into her to provide resistance as she pushes. But fair warning: Don't ever brag that you were part of the birthing process!

CUT THE CORD

You might never get to cut the ceremonial ribbon at the opening of a new super-market—those frat pictures floating around the internet will get in the way of any political run, after all—but you can do one better. Cutting the umbilical cord is a profound way for the father to get truly involved inside the delivery room.

Cutting the cord is a modern-day tradition. It has replaced the old trope of the new father huddling with his besties in the waiting room to puff a congratulatory stogie blithely unaware of the chaos that has just occurred 10 yards away. Cord-cutting is a simple thing, but there are few crucial need-to-knows before you rush in with industrial shears in hand, just so you don't wind up being unpleasantly surprised. First there are certain circumstances that will preclude you cutting anything. These include a cesarean birth, a semi-emergency situation in which the cord needs to be cut to get the baby out, and certain natural childbirth processes, like a *lotus birth*, where you wait for the placenta and cord to detach naturally of their own accord.

The umbilical cord was the baby's food and blood supply. It's attached at one end to what will become your offspring's belly button, and to the placenta stuck on the side of your life partner's womb. Cutting the cord is a symbolic act making your kid a citizen of the outer world, no longer connected to the womb.

Normally the medical pro will clamp the cord close to the baby, and on the placenta. You'll cut between these two clamps. The cord should have stopped pulsing, indicating that no blood is still flowing in the line. Arm yourself with a sturdy pair of scissors and a pad of gauze to catch any blood drips and start cutting. You'll find the cord is unusually tough and will take some effort to sever. But once you're through, the baby is an untethered human, ready to begin the rest of his or her life as an independent person. Yikes!

GIVE YOUR INFANT A SPONGE BATH

A dirty infant is a potentially sick infant, and Papa, you don't want a sick newborn. Unfortunately newborns are also a little delicate and can't have a regular tub or sink bath until the umbilical cord stub falls off. The solution? A sponge bath (no sponge actually needed).

Gather everything first: soft, soft towels; cotton balls; washcloth and mild soap meant for newborns; new diaper; and a clean set of clothes. Mix lukewarm water with a small amount of the soap in a bowl. Babies are hypersensitive to cold, being wet, or discomfort. Keep your little one bundled up in a towel, exposing and cleaning—then drying—one part at a time before moving on.

Start with the head and be as gentle as you possibly can. Use cotton balls on more sensitive areas such as around the eyes, mouth, ears, and genitalia. Work from the top down, using the washcloth on large areas of skin and finishing at the genitals and bottom. Make sure the baby is entirely dry before dressing him or her and then take a moment to breathe in that euphoric clean-baby smell.

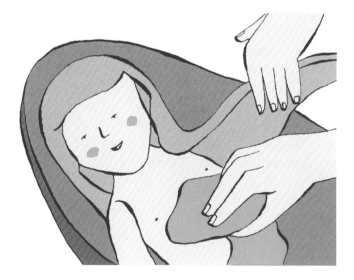

CLIP YOUR BABY'S NAILS

A freshly minted baby presents a bad combination: knife-sharp, fast-growing nails and impulsive movements. They end up cutting themselves as they grab at that face, and those cuts can easily get infected. That's why it's so important to keep baby's toe and fingernails trimmed. The trouble is, thems some tiny nails. And as you'll soon discover, babies don't dig having their hands controlled. So here's the lowdown on getting the claws trimmed with a minimum of fuss and fallout.

Pick your moment. The best time is when the baby is asleep or as calm as possible (such as right after a bath, when the nails are also super soft). The first time, work with your partner, who can distract the baby and help isolate digits. Use baby scissors with a rounded tip or baby nail clippers. With scissors, cut each nail slowly but confidently, in one go without leaving jagged lines. With clippers, take three bites, removing a third of the nail each time. Move carefully and slowly and stay clear of the nail bed. Better to leave a nail slightly long than cause a wound that can become infected. A toy in the opposite hand is a great distraction during the process.

PREP A BOTTLE OF FORMULA

Who doesn't like occasionally hitting the bottle? Many of us do—and so do babies. But for your little whelp, going to the bottle is a whole nother thing. Some kiddos just never take to a breast (what could they possibly be thinking?), and most moms move a baby off the breast after six months anyway. In between that oh-so-wonderful mom's milk and those oh-so-disgusting mashed carrots and peas lies a period of formula feeding. That's both great news and less great news. The good part? Bottles free up Mom and make feeding time much easier. But ingesting anything is a simple way for baby bumble to get sick. That's why the process of preparing formula is aimed at avoiding any physical repercussions, from spit-up to viral infections.

Start with the gear. Bottles and nipples must be absolutely clean, which can mean boiling them or, at the very least, a thorough cleaning with strong soap and a complete rinsing with scalding water (follow your pediatrician's recommendations).

The formula (or "busy parent's miracle mix" as it's more aptly known) needs to be handled like the precious commodity it is. Always check the expiration date and never use expired formula or any container that has been open for more than a month. Store unmixed formula in a cool, dry place—never in the refrigerator. Mixed formula should always be refrigerated when not being used immediately and should be discarded after twenty-four hours. Don't freeze prepared formula or leave it out to come to room temperature.

To prepare the formula, wash your hands thoroughly. Boil the water and let it cool until lukewarm. Add the water to the bottle and then add a level scoop of formula for every two ounces (59 ml) of water (unless the label specifies otherwise). Put the cap on the bottle and shake vigorously until entirely mixed. Replace the cap with the nipple and feed your hungry formula monster or store immediately in the refrigerator (the bottle, not the baby).

To be safe, toss any formula the baby doesn't finish within a half hour. It's contaminated with the child's saliva, which basically makes the bottle a petri dish for bacteria.

LIMIT DIAPER STANK

Hard to adore your fresh little angel with the smell of dirty diapers filling your house? Even salt-of-the-earth parents would rather keep the unique smell from floating like a permanent toxic cloud into every room. Never fear: Strong smells like baby poo can seem intractable, but there are ways to defeat them!

Isolation is key. Set up the changing table in a room with cross ventilation if possible and limit diaper changes to that room. Keep a lidded diaper pail right by the changing table and use deodorant liners or pucks in the pail or even sprinkle baking soda in the bottom. Be aware that there may come a day when the smell and that pail are just inextricably intertwined, in which case, the pail needs to go.

Clean your changing station after every change, with a baby-safe organic cleaner. Your best defense against pervasive dirty-diaper smell will be getting the offending object out of the house; empty the trash and diaper pail each night. As a last resort, try changing diaper brands; some are just more odor-absorbent than others.

BOND WITH BABY

Dads didn't get the experience of a physical connection with their baby, so they can be less bonded with the baby than the mother naturally is. Don't resign yourself to the garage—there are lots of tricks to bond intimately with your baby and become mommy the second.

Simple snuggling and cuddling go a long way in the bonding battle. The more close contact you have with little bug, the more he or she gets familiar with your smell and your voice. Looking into an infant's eyes is a keyhole to the universe. Okay, maybe not. But it's a fantastic and natural way to connect. Even more so if you're rocking in a rocking chair.

Skin-to-skin contact is invaluable for reinforcing intimacy, and a half hour spent lying on the couch bare chested with your baby in only a diaper can be a pretty special lead-up to a nap or just tremendously pleasant quiet downtime.

SWADDLE A BABY

Babies are weird. They go through this big trauma to exit the womb, find themselves in a huge wonderful world ripe for exploring, and what do they want? To be bound up just as they were in the womb. Weirdos.

Fortunately, you can accommodate them by wrapping them up tightly. Called "swaddling," this is normally reserved for very young infants. Depending on the child, swaddling can help the baby sleep or even calm a fussy baby. It's not a new invention; babies have been swaddled for thousands of years. These days, the pros caution against overuse because the traditional method of swaddling—which keeps the baby's legs straight, stiff, and confined—can lead to hip disorders. But you can finesse that.

To swaddle your baby, you're going to need a clean, soft baby blanket. Nope, not that throw that's been parked on the back of the couch and definitely not the 100-count sheet from your extra set that you reserve for guests you don't like. Lay the blanket down on a clean surface, such as the top of your bed, in a diamond formation. Fold down the top point of the diamond so that you make a straight edge about 2 feet (61 cm) across. Lay the baby on the blanket, face up, with his or her shoulders right below the straight-line fold.

Hold the baby's arm (usually, right-handed people start with the left side of the baby) and fold one side of the blanket snugly over the arm and tuck the edge under the opposite side of the baby, leaving the opposite arm free. Ensuring the baby's legs are able to move in the hip sockets, bend out to the sides and at the knee, fold the bottom of the blanket "diamond" up to make a mini triangle of the unfolded side. Now fold over the unfolded side, snugly holding the second arm against the baby's body and tuck the blanket into a seam made by the previous folds, behind the baby. If you're putting the baby to sleep swaddled, only lay bumble on his or her back—never his or her stomach or side.

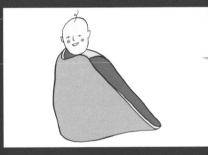

CARRY A NEWBORN

The big challenge with holding newborns is that they have no neck strength. (Seriously, they were so busy in the womb that there was no time to do a few neck exercises?) That means no matter what hold you use to carry a newborn, you have to ensure the head and neck are both fully supported.

As long as the baby is secure and comfortable, any hold will work. But a couple have distinct benefits, and any hold should be comfortable for you as well. Among the most common is the *shoulder hold.* One arm supports the baby's bottom while the free hand supports the head and neck and secures the baby's face against your shoulder. Unfortunately this one doesn't really allow the baby to see a lot.

The cradle is great for staring into your newborn's eyes. Lay the baby in the crook of one elbow and run the other arm parallel to help support the side and the head of the baby. Flip the script of the shoulder hold to let people see your baby by grasping him by the crotch and wrapping your free arm across his chest and neck—called the *hello hold* for obvious reasons.

A good way to deal with gas (the baby's, not yours) is the *football hold.* Drape the baby over your forearm as you would carry a football if you were running for the end zone. Use your free hand to stabilize the back and head, and the pressure against the baby's stomach will help ease the discomfort of the gas. Okay it will help the kid fart.

A more intimate hold—not really a carry—is the *lap hold.* Sit down and make a tent of your knees and lay the baby along your lap with the head on the seam between your knees. The baby will face you, and you're hands will be relatively free to tickle or play with the baby.

Shoulder Hold

Cradle Hold

Hello Hold

Football Hold

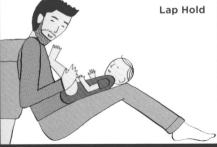

Lap Hold

CORRECTLY BURP A BABY

Your newborn will love to eat (a chip off the old block, that one) but they aren't very good at it. In fact, they often swallow as much air as food and then become very unhappy when their tiny stomachs mimic a balloon. Even though you are a world champion belcher—the entire alphabet, you say?—it's going to take a while and some practice for your beloved offspring to follow in your footsteps and do you proud. In the meantime, you'll have to help him or her get the air out.

Burp the baby right after breastfeeding and halfway through—and at the end of—bottle feeding. There are two basic techniques: The most common is to put a towel or cloth over your shoulder and then hold the baby facing behind you flat against your shoulder, patting the baby's back gently but firmly. The other method is to seat the baby sideways on one leg as you're seated, cradle the baby's jaw in your free hand, and pat his back with the other. Don't worry if you don't get a burp every time, it'll happen.

BATHE YOUR NEWBORN IN A TUB

You'll know it's time to transition from sponge baths to baby's first real bath when the umbilical stump falls off and the belly button fully heals. The trick to a calming, successful infant bath is temperature control. Infants are still developing their internal temperature-control mechanisms; avoid extremes of hot or cold.

The water should be between 90°F (32°C) and 110°F (43°C); use a thermometer rather than your judgment. Turn up your home's temp to ensure the baby doesn't get cold while wet. The water in the infant tub should be shallow, no more than two inches (5.1 cm).

Undress the baby quickly and slide him into the water. Keep him comfortable by covering exposed skin with warm washcloths as you wash the rest of the baby. Sudsing up the bumble isn't necessary. Warm water and a soft washcloth are usually all the cleaning power you'll need. If you opt for soap or shampoo, use mild products meant for infants and avoid contact with eyes or mouth. As soon as you're done, dry and wrap that clean angel up in a soft, warm towel. When your prince is completely dry, dress him.

STOP A BABY FROM FUSSING

Until your infant is about six weeks old, crying is the only way he has of effectively communicating (kind of like your boss and complaining). But added to the burden of adjusting to parenthood and big-time sleep deprivation, a shrill baby's cry can easily wear parents' nerves thin. So first and foremost, chill. Take a deep breath and call for help if you're at wit's end. Never shake a baby, crying or otherwise. Yelling at a crying child who lacks the language skills to even understand you only makes matters worse. Frustration coupled with exhaustion is the enemy of good parenting.

Next look for the most obvious source of the baby's distress. Change the diaper, check for a fever or other signs of sickness, and feed a hungry baby (or burp the little one). If you can't find an obvious cause, the crying may be a result of overstimulation, excessive fatigue, or something more subtle. That's when you turn to plan B strategies.

First up try swaddling that child. Swaddling makes babies feel more secure and safe and can often quiet them. Holding the baby lying down on his side can also be effective, although switch him to his back if he starts to fall asleep. Motion can also be soothing to infants, which is why many parents discover that sitting bumble in a secured car seat on top of a washing machine switched on, or taking him for a long car ride, can be a simple cure-all for a fussing baby. The same goes for white noise. Sometimes all it takes is the sound of a hair dryer or white-noise machine to calm the little bundle of nerves. If all else fails, you may want to try a pacifier, because the sucking reflex can have a powerful calming influence on a baby.

The last resort is to call the doctor. Even if the doctor can find nothing wrong, you'll have the reassurance that there is not a serious medical issue at play. Maintain your sanity by keeping in mind that one day soon, you'll be playing happily with this human siren you're carrying around.

DIAPER LIKE A PRO

If there's one thing any baby is expert at, it's filling a diaper. You're going to change about a bazillion, so you might as well become a pro out of the gate and make it easy on yourself.

Start by staging. Set up a changing table equipped with diapers, a diaper pail, wipes, lotion or powder, and a padded, cleanable changing surface. Lay the baby face up on the surface, with a new diaper open underneath the baby's bum. Loosen the old diaper, holding the baby's ankles up with one hand. Leave it draped over the unmentionables for twenty seconds; cold air causes a pee reflex in babies.

Once clear, lift the bottom up and clean it thoroughly with a wipe. Breathe through your mouth as you slide the soiled diaper out and close the adhesive tabs before dropping it in the diaper pail. Lower the baby's squeaky-clean butt down on the new diaper. Close the tabs tightly enough to contain any leakage but loose enough to allow for free movement and circulation. Congrats! You are now a diaper-changing machine.

DEAL WITH A COLICKY BABY

You've climbed sheer walls, cliff dived, raced your motorcycle through tightly wound S curves—you're a manly man, sure. But the mere word *colic* can bring a shudder down your spine. You're generally fearless, but every man-dad has his limits.

If your infant becomes afflicted with colic, you can give up on sleeping right now. Unless you have a perfect agreement and trade-off with a steel-nerved significant other, you are both going to forgo anything resembling restorative sleep for weeks. The good news? It's only weeks at worst. The mysterious condition—marked by persistent low-grade pain for the baby expressed through persistent and long bouts of crying—rarely goes beyond the third month of life, and most babies will be through it within three to four weeks. Three to four *long* weeks.

Not every strategy works, but it's good to have a number of them in your parenting tool kit. Plopping your personal alert system into a chest carrier so that the baby faces out and then going for a walk (even if it's around the inside of the house) is a frequently used and often successful technique.

There can be a digestive system component to colic, so stomach-easing techniques can have a big impact. The "colic carry" is similar to the football hold; lay the baby stomach-down along your forearm with the head in your palm to soothe the baby's stomach. You can also place a warm washcloth on the baby's tummy to help with pain, and laying her on her back and pedaling her leg can relieve excess gas. As an alternative, lay her across your legs as you're seated and gently massage her back.

Colic can sometimes be eased by changing the baby's formula or, if she's being breastfed, by changing the mother's diet away from anything spicy or strong, such as garlic and onions. The feeling of motion can provide temporary relief, so a long car ride or even putting the baby in a carrier and securing it in place on top of a running washer or dryer can work (keep ahold of the carrier so that it doesn't vibrate off the unit).

CLEAN BABY'S TEETH

Sooner or later that toothless love bundle is going to start growing her first set of chompers. Even though these "baby teeth" are placeholders for adult teeth, they need care, too—and none too soon. This is especially true as babies are introduced to fruit juices and strained fruits that expose nascent teeth to sugar.

There are two reasons to begin toothbrushing early. First by keeping baby teeth healthy, you head off health problems and unnecessary infant distress and lay a good foundation for adult teeth. Decay in baby teeth can also lead to difficulties in chewing or learning to speak. Second you expose your baby to a beneficial lifetime habit.

Because gum health is intertwined with tooth health, baby dental care actually begins even before the first teeth pop up. Moisten a soft, clean washcloth or a fine gauze pad with warm water and wipe down the gums. Do this twice a day right after feedings or before bedtime.

Once the new teeth make their appearance, it's time to start using a brush and a tiny amount of toothpaste. You'll start, just as you do with any important project, by making sure you have the right gear. When it comes to cleaning an infant's teeth, that means a toothpaste meant for babies and a very soft-bristled toothbrush intended for baby teeth. The toothbrush should have a short, fat handle.

Brush the bumble's teeth twice a day, preferably right after feedings. Make it fun so that your child forms a positive image of the exercise; sing, laugh, or create a game out of brushing. A brightly colored toothbrush also adds to the experience for the baby.

For infants, a dab of toothpaste about the size of a grain of rice will be plenty. Older infants can move to one the size of a pencil eraser (the brushing motion will do most of the cleaning). Use a circular motion to brush all teeth surfaces and the gums, front and back. Remember to be gentle and don't rush. Be careful of the baby moving his head. Brush the teeth and gums for about two minutes to thoroughly clean them.

HELP YOUR LITTLE ONE WALK

Yeah, okay, it's not making the varsity squad in high school. But one of the most significant and exciting hallmark moments in your child's development is walking. You can play an important part in helping that baby take his first steps and beyond.

You'll know that your tyke is ready when he pulls himself up at a coffee table or chair and stands and bounces on his legs. He may even attempt letting go and stepping. Don't worry about counting months; every kid walks only when the individual is ready. For some little ones, that happens before their first birthday. Others may take eighteen months to get mobile. When your baby starts showing signs, take steps to help the development.

First and most important, recheck your childproofing to ensure every room is still safe from the higher perspective of a walking baby. Keep cords out of reach because you don't want your wobbly little guy grabbing for a lamp cord in an effort to remain upright. Buy safety gates for stairs. You should also keep your baby barefooted in the house as much as possible. Socks equal slipping, which is good for a laugh but not so much for coordination development. Baby shoes are just downright restrictive. Use soft flexible shoes or grip booties when letting your tot strut outside.

Stay away from wheeled walkers. They seem like a good idea but can delay the process of your infant learning to balance on his own. You can introduce weighted push toys like a toy lawnmower (training for chores!) as a way for your baby to legitimately practice walking distances.

Stand over your child, holding his hands up and following him as he takes tentative steps. If he lets go of one side to test out his independence, let him—but keep your hand at the ready for him to grab again. As the child becomes better at aided locomotion, let him walk alongside his stroller for some part of the daily constitutional. And don't feel bad about dreaming of him breaking around the edge on a pass option play.

TRIM AN INFANT'S HAIR

Maybe you dig the shaggy, hipster look for your locks. But for your baby? Long hair only spells trouble. It becomes a collector of mashed and lost food, a sweeper gathering dust bunnies and cobwebs, and it presents the chance to get your kiddo stuck in buttons on clothing or snagged on furniture or toys. The long and short of it is, infants don't benefit from the hipster look.

As your baby grows, so grows his hair, and it will eventually need a quick trim. This isn't a total haircut (babies ain't got time for that!). First collect the tools: Grab a pair of shears, two big bibs, a small spray bottle filled with warm water, an infant comb, and your kid's favorite toys. Make your move when he is happy and content—right after a nap or feeding—to limit protest. Secure the baby in a high chair with a belt and give him a toy. If your little charge is not fond of being belted into a chair, you can rope Grandma or Grandpa into holding the little one in place on their lap.

Make happy noises like it's fun time. Slip on the bibs front and back or wrap a towel around the baby's shoulders (bibs are easier because they won't slide off).

Once the baby is preoccupied with the toy, spray the areas you're going to cut with the warm water. Work quickly because you never know when your window of opportunity will start collapsing. Gently pull a small section of hair to be cut between two fingers (in the "barber's grip") and snip off the ends following the plane of your fingers. Let go of the hair and move to a new section. If the bumble gets fussy, swap in a new toy. When you think you've got the worst of it, comb out the hair and check for long strands you missed the first time around. Clean up the cut as necessary.

Always remember that babies don't go to clubs, so stopping a trim in the middle of the process due to baby hysterics is no big deal; you can always finish up later.

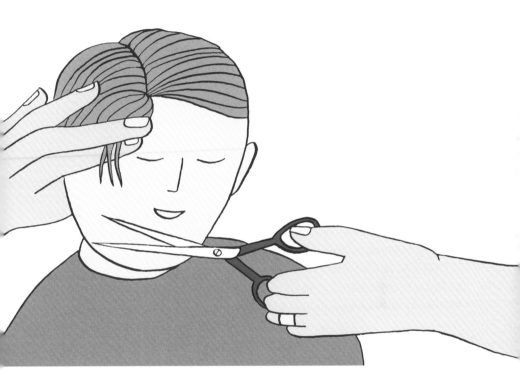

KEEPING BABY BUNDLED

Once you have to take your child with you out into the heartless Minnesota winter or into the brutal gales of a New England December, you'll second-guess that decision not to move to Los Angeles. Unfortunately it's too late. Now you have to become an expert on bundling up your infant to head off everything from ear infections to plain old discomfort.

The big challenge is the car seat. If you bundle up the baby in a bulky snowsuit so that she looks like a cutout of a mini Eskimo, you won't be able to properly tighten the harness in the car seat and little peanut will be less than totally safe. Better to dress the baby in lighter layers and then cover her in the car seat with a blanket.

The big rule is never to bundle a bumble so completely that you cover the face. Breathing trumps staying warm, and it won't hurt the baby to have a little cold air on her face. Whatever you dress your baby in, it should not force the child's chin to chest or otherwise restrict breathing. You should also be able to always see your little one's face, to judge if the baby is in any distress.

The extremities are a little different. In cold weather, it's exceptionally important to keep a baby's feet, hands, and head covered. A hat is always in order, as are gloves and warm booties or similar footwear.

A stroller has different rules than a car seat. If you're headed out for a walk on a brisk day, a snowsuit for the baby is perfectly acceptable. If the suit does not cover the hands, make sure you slip mittens on the little one. (And, as a rule, stay away from mittens or any clothing with strings because they represent a possible strangulation hazard.) If the child is adept at pulling mittens off, feel free to use heavy wool socks over her hands instead. They go up much further on the arm and are difficult for a little child to pull off.

CAPTURE BABY'S PRECIOUS MOMENTS

There is certainly something to be said about our modern digital times. Photographing anything once meant careful framing and lens adjustment and a long wait as photos were processed. Only when you got them back did you discover that your thumb was over the lens the whole time. A digital camera or smartphone allows you take an unlimited number of shots, editing or deleting those that don't accurately capture your memories. Video is much easier as well, and most phones will do a great job of filming baby's first steps or other milestones.

Start with the Boy Scout motto: Be prepared. If you have a high-quality phone, the camera is probably excellent. Make sure you keep it nearby. If not, set out your camera where you spend most of the time with the baby. That way, you'll know where it is when your tyke goes on a smiling jag or takes a shot at saying, "Daddy."

If you're at a loss as to what to shoot, you can stage shots as well as grabbing the spontaneous moment here and there. A good place to start is marking monthly progressions with a series of photos. Sit the baby up in the same chair or on the same couch during the same day each month. Tape up a piece of paper with the baby's age on it, and you'll be recording development as it occurs. Past the age of one, you may want to do shoots every six months or every year.

A few simple techniques will ensure that you get more good shots than duds. Get down on the baby's level for more intimate photos. Don't be afraid to use the black-and-white setting on your phone or camera for more stylish portraits and use indirect lighting. When the baby is directly lit—by a window or with a flash—the strong light can create annoying "hot spots" in the final photo. If you're using a flash, bounce it off a reflective surface rather than shooting it directly at the baby (bumbles aren't particularly fond of flashes going off in their faces anyway).

RECOGNIZE AN EAR INFECTION

Just as crabgrass is the bane of your perfect lawn, ear infections are the bane of your perfect child. Ears are complex structures prone to malfunction in developing humanoids. Children are especially susceptible to inner-ear problems, most of which can cause pain and hearing issues. Childhood ear infections involve fluid trapped behind the eardrum, in which bacteria proliferate. The infection causes painful swelling in the sensitive tissues of the inner and middle ear. Chronic repeat infections can lead to long-term damage and other conditions, such as fluid becoming trapped behind the eardrum on a more permanent basis, which may require minor surgery to relieve.

Recognizing and identifying an ear infection can require a dad to be part mind reader. The pain and symptoms mimic a lot of things—from colic to overstimulation to mystery sicknesses. But there are distinct, if subtle, signs particular to an ear infection.

The baby will pull at one ear repeatedly. As an infection progresses, your kiddo will also fuss incessantly and the pain may be worse if the child tries to eat. Fluid draining from the ear is a rather obvious symptom but is far rarer than a fever, difficulty sleeping, and inability to hear on one side.

Fortunately the solution is easy and it's called amoxicillin. This antibiotic is taken for seven to ten days, usually through a dropper (and is flavored appealingly like bubble gum). Your bumble will be happy and pain free inside of two days, but you'll need to give him the whole course of the antibiotic or risk bigger problems.

If you know your pediatrician well and he or she knows your baby, he or she may be able to diagnose the ear infection over the phone and save you a trip to the office. Although repeat episodes are common due to the anatomy of the young inner ear, you can take steps to limit further ear infections. Don't put the baby to bed with a bottle, never expose your baby to cigarette or vape smoke, follow the vaccine schedule your pediatrician recommends, and keep your child away from other sick children as much as possible.

MANAGING NEW MOM MOOD SWINGS

Ah, you poor simple man, you. You thought that as soon as you got bumble home, into the fold as one happy little family, that mood swings and puzzling outbursts would all be behind you. Wishful thinking, Papa. Time to think again.

The hormonal tsunami rages on for new moms. They may have wild ups and downs and periods of near immobility. They may even slide into true postpartum depression. Because it's not enough just to have your life upended by a nine-pound bundle of concerns and unpredictability, that's why.

Your wife may be able to temporarily rally for visitors, which means you're the one who is most likely to figure out something ain't right. Although sleep deprivation can take a toll on all of us, problematic mood swings and—most devastatingly—the onset of postpartum depression, are a different animal, one that often requires medication, therapy, or both.

Start with the signs. They can include a profound sadness, lack of desire to care for the baby, frequent crying jags without obvious cause, irrational irritability that can slide into rage, skewed eating habits (much more than usual or much less), lack of interest in otherwise fun activities, avoidance of interpersonal contact with friends or family and the baby, difficulties concentrating and memory disruption, and even thoughts of harming herself or the baby.

Let's be clear here: It's a tumultuous time. As new parents, you are both dealing with big issues, profound life changes, and justifiable concerns about the future. Any mother can experience a fairly normal adjustment period called the "baby blues." But those symptoms are mild in comparison and go away in two to three weeks. If things seem to be getting worse, get on the horn and call for medical backup.

Obviously the symptoms can be broad and vague and—given that you're missing the medical degree your mom wanted you to get—depression can only be truly diagnosed and properly treated by a medical professional. Even if your wife fights the idea, you need to go to bat for all three of you and get her help.

SAVE A BABY FROM CHOKING

You, sir, are never just a bystander. You are Johnny-on-the-spot. That includes being ready to save the most precious member of your family in the rare event of an emergency. That means knowing how to rescue your baby if she starts choking.

Just as with an adult, if the baby can still cough, breathe, and make noise, hold her and let her try to dislodge the obstruction by coughing it out. If, at any point, she stops being able to make sounds or is apparently not breathing, immediately call 911.

Then jump into action. Position bumble in an adapted football hold, along your forearm, with her head lower than her chest. This is going to be a little awkward but support the baby's head with your palm, stabilizing it against your thigh. Be sure that you're not blocking the mouth or twisting the neck.

This is the hard part: Using the heel of your open hand, strike the baby's back, right between her shoulder blades, five times, as if you were firmly pushing someone away. You want to thrust firmly enough to dislodge any obstruction but not so hard that you actually cause damage to the baby.

If after five thrusts the blockage is not dislodged, move on to plan B. Flip the baby faceup but still with the head lower than the chest. Use three fingers to press along the nipple line at the breastbone. Thrust five times quickly or until the object comes out. While the baby is still conscious, repeat the entire process until the object is dislodged or the baby loses consciousness. At that point call 911, if you haven't already done so. Then attempt to clear the throat with your fingers (your wife's may be smaller and more able to do this if she is on the scene) but don't stick a finger all the way down the throat if you can't easily pinch the blockage or you'll push it more firmly into the windpipe. Begin baby CPR and continue until the little one can breathe on her own or the paramedics arrive.

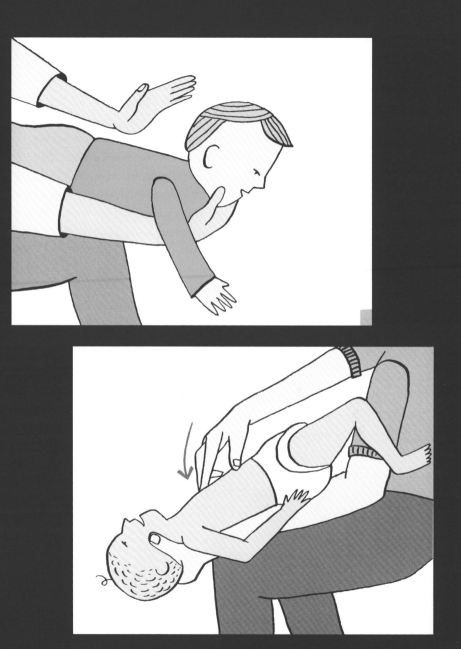

CHECK YOUR NEWBORN'S REFLEXES

Testing reflexes is a great way for any dad to reassure himself of normal baby development and can be a fun way of witnessing the funky ways a developing neurological system works.

Stroke the edge of the baby's mouth to start the *root reflex*, which helps babies find a nipple. Similarly, stroke the roof of your infant's mouth and he'll latch onto your finger thanks to the *suck reflex* (helping him get milk from a nipple). The *startle reflex* is a response to a loud noise or even the baby's own cry, where he flings out his arms and jerks his head in surprise. Every parent's joy is the *grasp reflex*, in which the baby grabs a finger stroking his palm. The *tonic neck reflex* is caused by turning your newborn's head to one side: The arm on that side straightens while the opposite one bends at the elbow. Doctors test for the *Babinski reflex*, which involves stroking the sole of the foot to make the toes spread and stretch. For pure amusement, try the step or *dance reflex*; hold the baby upright with his feet resting on a solid surface and he should do a happy dance!

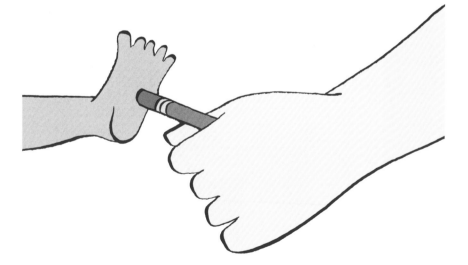

NO-FUSS MEDICINE DELIVERY

Here's the good news. The pharmaceutical industry long ago realized that babies aren't going to take pills, no way, no how. The bad news? Babies aren't much better at sucking down liquid medicine, especially when they ain't feeling good. And when the baby ain't feeling good, the dad ain't going to feel good.

Any parent who has tried to get a dropper full of antibiotic syrup down his little one's throat when the infant is tired and suffering with an earache can attest to just how imperfect that delivery method might be. Never fear: There is a better way.

You can fill your baby's favorite bottle nipple with a dropperful of medicine. (You can also buy special dispensers with nipple heads, but why go through the extra expense?) If that doesn't do the trick because the taste of the medicine is just too unappealing, try cloaking the medicine in a dollop of chocolate syrup—a substance especially good at hiding flavors. However, don't feed chocolate syrup to babies younger than six months.

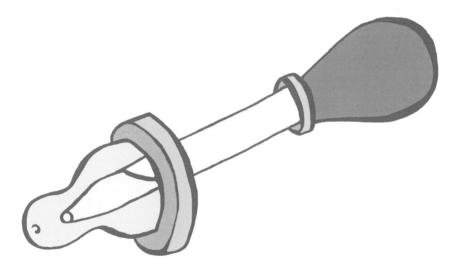

HOW TO MASSAGE YOUR BABY

Bet you didn't know that the spa experience can benefit your bouncing baby. A massage may help your little one sleep better, can ease some symptoms of colic, and cements the bond between you and your bumble. Best of all, it's easy—no special training required.

All you'll need is some baby oil or massage oil specifically formulated for infants, a plastic changing mat or comfortable soft and cleanable surface, a new diaper, and a clean soft towel. Test the massage oil beforehand on a tiny patch of the baby's skin to ensure there is no allergic reaction. Choose your moment carefully; don't attempt a massage right before or after feeding. You want the baby to be as happy and content as possible. You'll also want to stop the massage if she becomes distressed or agitated. Spend no more than five to ten minutes on the massage.

Lay the baby on her back, on the changing pad on the floor or other low, stable surface. Put a few drops of oil in the palms of your hands and warm them by rubbing them together. Start with the feet and use your thumb pad to gently rub from heel to toe several times. Work your way to the legs and, while holding a foot, rub up the leg toward the hip. Stretch and bend the legs.

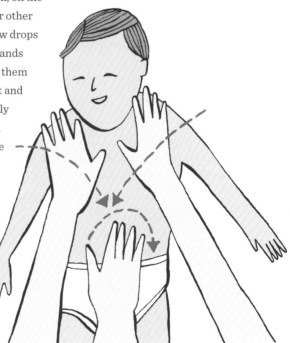

Move on to the torso. Lightly rub from each nipple out in an arc to the point of each shoulder. Rub down each arm and then carefully massage the stomach by making an upside horseshoe from one side to the other. Avoid the diaphragm and use only very light pressure. This can be the most sensitive area on the baby.

Finish by lightly rubbing the face from the top of the head (avoid any contact with the crown), down in an arc on each side to the corners of the mouth. If your snuggle buddy is still calm and in a good mood, flip her over and massage from the base of the neck, down the spine to the butt. When you're done, wrap her in the towel and use it to wipe off the oil before dressing her.

AVOID SIDS

If there were a manual for parents, the first page would list the number one responsibility: Keep that little bundle alive. Sudden Infant Death Syndrome (SIDS) is a mysterious condition that works against the parental prime directive. Keeping SIDS far from your doorstep is first a matter of knowing the enemy.

SIDS is exactly what it sounds like: sudden, unexplained death of an otherwise apparently healthy baby. Premature babies, males, those with relatives who have died of SIDS, and any baby two to four months old are all more susceptible. But you can take steps to protect your lovely bundle of joy.

Always put an infant to sleep on his back, in a crib with nothing else in it. Babies should not be overheated, and you should never cover an infant's face in sleeping or bundling them for the outdoors. It's wisest—for at least the first six months—to have the baby sleep in your room so you can detect any distress as soon as it happens. It's also great if your baby can be breastfed for at least six months, which has been shown to reduce the risk of SIDS. Using a pacifier may also have a preventative effect but don't force it on your child.

KNOW WHEN TO CALL THE DOCTOR

You may be a jack-of-all-trades in your home, but you also know when a plumbing problem is above your pay grade or when to take your car into the mechanic. That's because any man worth his salt knows when to call for backup, and that's never truer then when that man is a dad. Your baby's health is no place to play Mr. Know-It-All. Of course, you don't want to be the parent that cries wolf at the first sign of gas pains either. It's a fine line, made finer by parental sleep deprivation and worry over a fussing baby.

But there are guidelines to when a call to a pediatrician is merited. Fever is the most common alarm signal, but it's not a slam-dunk reason to dial the doctor. Remember that a baby's regulatory system is still in the process of maturing. They may quickly spike a relatively high fever that comes back down to normal within hours without any intervention. The alarm signal is a higher-than-normal fever coupled with other symptoms, including vomiting, lethargy, poor skin color, or difficulty breathing. Other signs that indicate you should make the call include sensitivity to light, a stomach that is painful when you touch it, diarrhea with a fever, an obvious rash, and any seizure (seizures are a reason to call 911).

Abdominal pain is one of the most difficult symptoms to deal with as a parent, because it can be very hard to know when to seek help or when to just wait for gas to pass or a disagreeable meal to be digested. Typically, if the baby has a hard or swollen stomach, or the entire midsection is very tender to the touch, it's time to call a doctor.

Vomiting and diarrhea are other symptoms that fall on a spectrum. If your child has been throwing up for several hours, can't keep even a sip of water down, or has diarrhea so bad that he is becoming dehydrated (dull skin, sunken eyes, unusual drowsiness, dry mouth) it's time to reach out to the pediatrician. Isolated instances of vomiting or diarrhea are a watch-and-wait situation.

SHARE A BED WITH BABY

Want to start a fistfight among childcare pros? Just mention the word *bedsharing* and stand back. Many organizations, like the American Academy of Pediatrics, take the position that parents should never sleep in the same bed with an infant because of the risk of SIDS. Others, like La Leche League, are more pragmatic and provide strict guidelines. In general you can share your bed as a matter of convenience; it's much easier for sleep-deprived mommies to do 2 a.m. breastfeedings in bed.

Your mattress must be firm not soft. Cover baby only with a light blanket, or none at all, and he should be lightly dressed. The baby has to sleep on his back and never on a pillow and must be otherwise healthy and a full-term infant. The mother should breastfeed in what's known as the "cuddle curl," with her arm as her pillow and her legs bent as if she were sitting, essentially surrounding and protecting the infant. If the mom has long hair, it should be captured in a hair tie or bun; and parents should never sleep with a baby if either of them has been drinking, has taken a sedative or sleep aid, is morbidly obese, or is a smoker.

HOW TO SAFELY CLEAN BABY'S EARS

Man, oh man, for such an important and hidden asset, a baby's ears are regularly ground zero for common infant ailments—most regularly, ear infections. But let's be clear here: Little bumble's ear-borne vulnerability rarely has anything to do with how clean her ears are.

There is some primeval compulsion to clean the inside of ears—our own and our children's. Resist that. Inside a baby's ears you'll find a fair amount of earwax, which is there as a protective barrier. Except in the case of a disorder, it will come and go of its own accord. Never get a cotton swab near a baby's ears. All you need is a cotton ball and washcloth. Using warm water, wet the cloth or cotton ball, and gently clean the outer ear. That's it, job done.

ALLEVIATE TEETHING PAIN

It's a mad irony that growing teeth is just about as painful as having them removed. But as an enlightened Dadskilled individual, you're not going to stand idly by while your child suffers through teething pain (and you and your better half suffer through lost sleep). You're going to slap new-tooth pain in the face.

To be accurate, the pain normally isn't in the teeth. It's in the gums that are being shredded as the teeth make their presence known. The solution is to lessen gum swelling and tenderness. The time-tested way to do that is with the power of cold. Teething biscuits and teething gel may offer some relief, but nothing is going to be so effective as something frozen.

Start with the simplest: a moistened washcloth kept in the freezer. Use a nubby washcloth because the texture will help relieve the gum irritation. Many parents quickly discover that freezing teething rings can have the same beneficial effect. Homemade ice pops add flavor into the mix (use organic juice!), but the trade-off is a huge mess. Frozen waffles are an even easier solution; they provide the relief of cold with a delicious, filling mush as they are chewed and warm up.

The most immediate relief may be Mom or Dad's (clean) finger, rubbed along the gums. Some parents put a small amount of liquor on the finger, but pediatricians and other professionals frown on this practice. They are also leery of home remedies such as clove oil or using other essential oils such as lavender or chamomile. It is hard to judge if the oil is irritating the gum or creating an adverse reaction, and no baby should be swallowing an essential oil.

A side effect of teething is drooling. Keep a cloth handy to clean up drool because over time, it can irritate the baby's skin. A short internet search will turn up many recipes for homemade teething creams and ads for complicated teething gloves and other devices. But simple solutions such as a frozen teething ring have proven their worth throughout history.

REMOVING NASAL MUCUS

Newborns don't have enough of a cough reflex to clear significant amounts of mucus. If and when they get sick and congested, you're going to have to clear little one's nose so he can breathe freely. The best removal method is with a bulb syringe. Make a mild saltwater solution by boiling a ¼ teaspoon (1.5 g) of table salt in 1 cup (237 ml) of water and letting it cool to room temp. Hold the bulb syringe in your palm, suck in some of the saltwater, and squirt a few drops up the

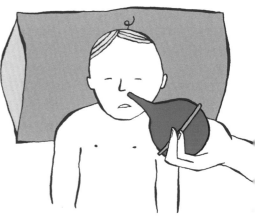

baby's nose to break up the mucus. Empty the syringe and collapse it. Carefully stick the tip up the baby's nostril at an angle. Let the bulb open to suction the mucus. Clean the syringe between suctionings in a bowl full of warm water. Do both nostrils, even if one is worse. When you're done, thoroughly clean the syringe with hot soapy water and a hot water rinse. Let it air-dry.

USE A RECTAL THERMOMETER

You infant is going to run a fever sooner or later. But if it's sooner, you're not going to be able to check the severity of the fever by taking his temperature in a traditional way. Any point before a baby is three months old, professionals advise taking a temperature rectally.

You'll use a regular digital thermometer (cleaning it thoroughly between uses with rubbing alcohol and hot soapy water), but you need to take the temperature with a minimum of trauma to the little one. Lay the baby on her back. Lubricate the tip of the thermometer with a liberal amount of petroleum jelly and carefully insert it into the rectum. Do not force it. Stop if you encounter resistance and try again. The tip should go in about ¾ inch (1.9 cm) for an accurate reading. Hold it in place until the thermometer signals a completed reading.

This stage is where the fun for a dad really begins.

CHAPTER 2

Dealing with Toddlers

Okay, it takes a lot to impress you. You've seen a drag race up close and personal. You've blazed your own trail, climbed your own mountains, been around and seen a lot of amazing things. But there is little to compare to watching the incredible development of your own toddler. It's like a fast-motion film of what learning is. That, sir, is the real deal.

This stage is where the fun for a dad really begins. Your offspring is absorbing new knowledge like a sponge, exploring and curious, beginning to speak actual words and giving back all that love you've been pouring into him.

That's some good stuff. But it also presents a set of challenges. Exploring his world means touching, inspecting, tasting, and smelling everything in the world— even unsafe stuff. It means climbing things that shouldn't be climbed and standing and bouncing on things that weren't made for standing and bouncing. It means going where he shouldn't go and taking apart things that are better left intact. The toddler stage, in short, adds a whole new urgency to the terms *childproofing* and *supervision*.

All that intellectual wonder and pure energy (oh boy, that energy) is interesting, amusing, and exhausting in equal parts. Ever try to chase a headless chicken or greased pig? If you have, then you have some idea of what it's like to follow and police a busy toddler over the course of his day. These little creatures are deceptively fast and can easily get into things you would never have imagined they could have accessed. But take a deep breath, keep your cool, and you can head off any potential danger and still help your toddler grow, learn, and develop like a champ.

The secret to managing the toddler years, as with so many childhood stages, is to be prepared. Knowing what type of curve balls your tiny TNT can throw you is the first step in handling whatever situation comes up. This chapter covers the entire spectrum, from how to keep the inquisitive young mind entertained (and out of trouble!) to addressing a potentially dangerous situation to breaking bad habits before they have a chance to become established. So before your toddler wreaks havoc on the house, your nerves, and himself, turn the page and get yourself ready, Freddy.

HELP YOUR TODDLER SLEEP THROUGH THE NIGHT

The holy grail of parenting is getting that little tiny wonder to snooze a good six to eight hours. Achieving that is like winning the lottery and getting a small piece of your adult life back, which is why so many parents are shocked to find that their toddler has suddenly decided that sleep is an unnecessary diversion from the business of being a toddler.

First off, check the nap schedule. It may be that your toddler is sleeping too much during the day and isn't as tired out as he should be come bedtime. Theoretically toddlers require about ten to twelve hours of sleep a day. If they're getting four to six of that in naps, well, you do the math. Next check down your list of possible sleep disturbances: a minor infection, earache, anxiety about a new situation or person, or—worst-case scenario—toddler sleep apnea (requiring a visit to a specialist).

Your first line of defense is to . . . do nothing. When you're toddler cries out at night, don't necessarily rush in to comfort him. Wait a couple of minutes to see if the child settles himself back down to sleep. If that doesn't work, go into his room to comfort him but don't bring him into yours. Neither of you will sleep well sharing a bed, and it's not a habit you should get your toddler into. Instead comfort your toddler but keep him in his bed, rub his back or speak in a very low voice reassuringly.

You should also take steps to ensure that mid-sleep wakeups don't occur. A quiet, low-key bedtime ritual, such as a bath, or a calm, pleasant story is an excellent way to put your child on the express to Snoozeville. You can also try a white-noise machine or even a fan in the room. Ensure that the sleep environment is comfortable and stable—no outside motion-activated lights coming on as raccoons pillage your garbage or creaking of the window that is loose in its frame. And no matter how successful these strategies are, always keep in mind this is a stage and will pass soon enough.

HIRE A NANNY

Mom and Dad have good-paying jobs but not much parental leave. What to do? Well, you can turn to local daycare and stick with their sometimes-constrictive rules, or you could leverage your assets and hire a full-time professional.

Finding the right nanny is a matter of getting a reliable referral. You can go the networking route, posting on social media and asking friends, but that often leads nowhere. The most reputable source will be a nanny agency. (A general web search will turn up a host of them.)

From there, picking the best candidate is all about research. Check references and determine what types of families the person has worked for and what their credentials are in the first place—some have specialized training and a degree in a related field such as early childhood education. At the very least, your nanny should know infant CPR and have basic emergency training. Be ready to pay a pretty penny for your finalist; even if they aren't sleep-in, nannies still make a healthy living wage.

CHOOSE A DAYCARE PROVIDER

As if keeping your toddler happy and healthy wasn't enough, there comes a time you'll probably have to select a daycare. These days, many parents don't have the option of one them staying home with the kiddo, and daycare is the least expensive option for ongoing daily babysitting. ("Least expensive" doesn't mean cheap, Ace.)

When you go hunting for the right place, you'll be faced with two basic options: a daycare center and home daycare. Centers are businesses for better or worse. Home daycare can range from a dedicated sole proprietor to a stay-at-home mom trying to make a few extra bucks.

Just because a daycare center is a business doesn't make it necessarily better than home daycare. It's notoriously hard to turn a profit in the business, and centers are often forced to pay employees at the low end of the scale. In terms of child professionals, you often get what you pay for.

The variables are why doing your due diligence is essential. Regardless of where you get the referral, you need to dig deep into the daycare's reputation and policies because your toddler's health and safety are at stake. Start with whether you and your child prefer a larger, more formal setting or a smaller home environment. Then ask a lot of questions, including hours of operation (do they go long in case of a late pickup?) and holidays or vacation closings; certifications if any for both the business and individual providers; insurance (a must); number of kids per daycare provider; complete cost, including unintentional late pickup charge and food charges; references (find parents like you with the same-age child); childcare approach regarding educational opportunities; how they resolve conflicts; discipline procedures; child sickness policy; immunization policy; food and food allergy policies; staff screening and experience; separation by age group; and safety and security procedures.

Start your search months earlier than you need the daycare. Once you find a potential candidate, it's important to tour the facility. Check how happy and well supervised the children are and the cleanliness of the facility. Then get ready for major separation anxiety.

PICK A PRESCHOOL

You are Mr. Prepared. You would never run out of gas, and you don't head out on even a short hike without a compass and extra water. So why wouldn't you want your youngster to get a head start and be super ready for elementary school? The trick to that is finding just the right preschool, and that's all about using your eyes, ears, and judgment.

Take a morning to preview any school you're considering. Nothing replaces an in-person experience. Tours and visits are the best way to figure out if any preschool is *the* preschool. This is your child's introduction to schools, teaching, and class-rooms; so it should be as pleasurable as possible. Keep any eye out for the key factors that create an environment conducive to learning.

Connection. The adults in the school should be making an effort to communicate directly and profoundly with even their youngest charges, which means getting down to the children's eye level and speaking calmly and directly to the child in front of them.

Lesson-focused discipline. Teachers and administrators should not be punishing children but instead using inappropriate behavior as teachable moments and instituting simple humane remedies such as time-outs. Rules should be clear for children and parents.

Play-centered learning. Remember, this is a *pre*school. Many of the higher concepts introduced in elementary school are not appropriate for a preschool, and learning for toddlers and preschool-age children should revolve around playing to learn. There should be a sense of fun and exploration in each classroom, and the environment should fairly scream "little kids playing."

Active classrooms. Following on the above, toddlers should be engaged through activity and movement, because they have short attention spans and high energy levels in any case.

Also assess the general state of the facilities. Are they clean? Is the school certified through the state? Are the teachers? Are the classrooms kept fairly orderly (no broken toys, windows, furniture, or dilapidated fixtures)? Are safety features such as a fire extinguishers, smoke alarms, and safety gates apparent and in good working order? Remember that this is your kid's first step toward a top college—make sure it's stumble free.

MAKE A SUCCESSFUL PLAYDATE

Busy schedules, a complicated world, and new norms are today's reality. As a toddler's parent, sooner or later you're going to be faced with setting up a playdate. Might as well knock it out of the park and get your child's social life off to a great start.

A playdate has to be safe to be fun. That starts with double-checking your childproofing. It also means that you're going to have to be on top of things; a playdate requires more watchful supervision than your child alone. That said, you have to let things unfold in a more or less natural manner. Minor squabbles, kids being loud, and messes are all part of the process; let them run their course until and unless there is a chance someone might get hurt.

A little planning will help things go smoothly. Consult with the other parents to ensure the playdate is scheduled around naps and meal times. As much as possible, have duplicate toys on hand so no battles break out over possession. Make your life easier by scheduling dates with toddlers that have a natural affinity with your child (although a play date can be an opportunity to broaden your child's social horizons).

FIND THE RIGHT BABYSITTER

By the time you're ready to leave your toddler with a babysitter, you probably haven't had an adults-only night out in months. You've earned it, and you should enjoy it. Ensure your peace of mind on that outing by crossing the T's and dotting the I's when it comes to your babysitter search.

Start with recommendations. Friends with children who are the same age, parents you know from time in birthing classes, and childcare professionals are all likely to be good sources of potential candidates. Your favorite daycare workers may moonlight as babysitters, especially if they're fond of your little one. But expect to pay a premium for such experienced babysitting help. Even if they don't offer babysitting services themselves, daycare workers or preschool teachers are usually great sources for recommendations.

If you have a college nearby, post on bulletin boards or talk to the campus work-study office to find an early childhood development or teaching degree candidate. The bonus with students is that their schedules are usually flexible and they need the money.

When it comes time to interview a potential babysitter, know your essential requirements. Start with age. Although many organizations, such as the Red Cross, are comfortable with babysitters as young as thirteen, you may prefer a more mature teen. You should also discuss the rules of the house and payment—including any extra payment when and if you're late getting home.

Be aware that a good babysitter will inevitably be in demand and you'll do yourself a favor with a little bit of planning and booking the babysitter well in advance. When it comes to the actual evening out, make sure that you leave the babysitter with a neighbor's or family member's phone number, the cell number for both you and your wife, and instructions for what you consider an emergency and what you want done in the event of one. That not only helps the babysitter deal with any eventuality; it makes for a lovely evening free of distracting worries.

FEED A PICKY EATER

Feeding your child is a top-of-list dad responsibility. So when that independent creature rejects meal after meal, it can be frustrating. Fortunately there are many ways to deal with your fussy gourmand.

Model healthy eating. Include a variety of healthy foods in your diet and eat them with obvious pleasure.

Involve the kiddo in meal making. Toddlers won't be able to do a lot; but you can integrate them in mealtime prep by letting them stir, hand you ingredients, or wash vegetables.

Establish a routine. Serve meals at the same time every day so your toddler becomes hungry on a schedule.

Limit snacking. Eating between meals only increases food resistance.

Be texture sensitive. Sometimes cubed and roasted potatoes might work where mashed potatoes failed.

Cook fun. Make games out of meals or prepare all-in-one dishes like pita pizzas, resembling faces or favorite cartoon characters. Cut vegetables in unusual shapes and serve them with nutritious dips like hummus.

Resist negotiation. Don't offer rewards such as dessert for finishing a dinner or other meal; it sets up a very negative pattern. Good nutrition is its own reward.

Don't force it. A truly hungry child will certainly eat. Few parents have to worry about malnutrition.

TEACH BRUSHING TO A TUNE

You're a fun guy. You know how to tell a joke and keep the party going. Well, be a fun dad, too, if you want life lessons to be easy for you toddler. Start with bringing the fun to one of the most boring—and important—daily rituals ever invented: brushing teeth. You set your child up to avoid a lot of pain and frustration in later life by integrating this ritual seamlessly into his life. The big challenge, given the attention span of a toddler, is to get her to brush for long enough that it does the job.

That's where music comes in. Find a simple, fun song that your toddler likes and play it each night when it comes time to brush teeth. Children's songs are generally upbeat, which makes them the perfect accompaniment to tooth brushing. Most kids' songs last two to three minutes, ideal when it comes to cleaning teeth. Musical tastes change, so be prepared with an entire playlist of possible favorites to rotate in any given night of the week.

NEVER LOSE A TODDLER IN A STORE

Buddy, you aren't alone if you have that parental nightmare where you go to pick up a quart of milk with the kiddo, and suddenly she's not at your side. You run around like a chicken with your head cut off, but you simply can't find her. It's one of the worst feelings a parent can experience. Avoid it at all cost.

There are physical and electronic ways to do that. The most tangible method is to physically attach yourself to the child with a leash harness (a leash you hold connected to a vest-type harness on your child), or a less intrusive wrist leash (two hook-and-loop wristbands connected by a spring lead). You can also go high-tech with a geolocator—basically a pinging unit you can follow on your phone. Just slip the locator in one of your toddler's pockets (some come as wearables) and you need to only glance at your phone to know exactly where she is.

TODDLER-IZE THE BATHROOM

Seems like a safe place, but for an uncoordinated toddler, the bathroom presents a number of dangers. You'll be using it a lot with the little one, so best to be safe rather than sorry. And it's crucial that the little guy feel comfortable there once you head into that oh-so-hopeful phase of potty training.

Start with that bathtub. Being the smart dad you are, surely you know to never leave a toddler unattended in the bathtub. Even if only to answer a quick phone call. The tub also needs toddler-proofing in other ways. Consider the slick surface of any tub. Antiskid pads are a great addition to a bathtub a toddler regularly uses. You can find them in all kinds of delightful shapes and sizes, and you might as well pick some that will amuse the kiddo.

A floating animal thermometer (they come in rubber duckies and toy turtles among other characters) is a great way to ensure the water is never too hot. For younger toddlers, a faucet guard that blocks the child from turning on the faucets is a worthy addition to your bathroom safety lineup. Lastly a suction grip handle is a handy aid for little kids who often have trouble getting in and out of the tub, and a padded vinyl tub apron guard keeps toddlers from hurting themselves on the hard tub apron.

Beyond the tub, use a toilet lid lock to prevent accidental drowning and other less serious, but no less gross, mishaps. Vanity cabinet door safety latches are a must. Move any medications or cosmetics off the counter and into a medicine chest or somewhere else far out of the reach of your little one. Same goes for plugged appliances—keep them out of reach.

If you have a tiled bathroom floor or other surface that would be extremely slippery when wet, either incorporate a large rubber-backed bath mat for Mr. Toddler to stand on while you towel dry him or put down removable nonslip pads.

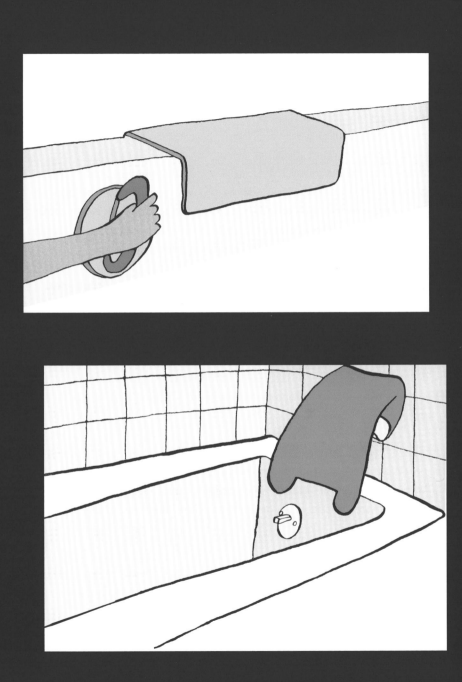

CREATE PIPE-CLEANER CREATURES

Lest you fall into the trap of thinking that taking care of your toddler is all heavy responsibilities and lost sleep, it's time you jumped into the pure fun to be had with your bumble. Amusing an older toddler is not hard, but the best fun activities are fun for a dad as well.

Count among those crafting with pipe cleaners. These multicolored, bendable, fuzzy sticks are available at craft stores and are super-easy to work with. Toddlers love the colors, and the cleaners require very little in the way of fine motor skills. That means dad can show off his creative skills to the amazement of the little one. Best of all, pipe cleaners don't create a mess or require much cleanup.

The best way to start out is a simple creature, such as a spider. An older toddler should have no problem following along with the instructions even if his spider may come out looking less like a spider and more like pipe-cleaner chaos.

1 Hold four cleaners in a bundle and bend in half.

2 Twist the bundle several times right below the bend, leaving a little circle that will serve as the head of the spider.

3 Continue twisting the bundle from the head down, to form a body.

4 Pull the body twist apart so there is a small opening and weave the end of each pipe cleaner through the opening, to create the legs.

5 Now kink the legs to create the leg joints. Form the body into a realistic shape and adjust as necessary. Bend the head up, perpendicular to the body. If you want to put the icing on the cake, glue googly eyes onto the head.

The wonderful thing about this creation is it takes about a minute to make. It is simple enough that, with a tiny bit of help, even a toddler can make his own spider. Throw a little imagination into the mix, and you'll be able to craft a T. rex, stick figure in any pose, simple reptiles and bugs, and even basic shapes like a heart or letters (help your toddler spell out "mom").

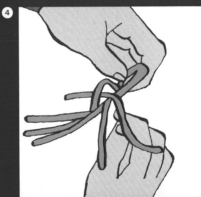

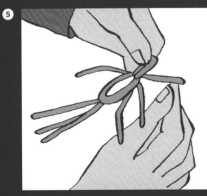

BUILD A SANDCASTLE

Show your toddler that you are king, at least of a temporary castle. Building a sandcastle is one of the most delightful parts of beach time for kiddos and grown-up kiddos. There's something magical about building a mini kingdom out of such an insubstantial material.

Ironically, to build the castle, you'll need to make that material slightly less insubstantial; dry sand does not a castle make. The sand you're working with should be just moist enough to hold together when squeezed in your hand. Too dry and it will fall apart; too wet and it will run through your fingers before it has a chance to set up.

As with all real estate, sandcastles are all about location. Choose a site not too busy or crowded, right about or slightly below the tide line that divides dark from light (dry) sand. You'll need nothing more than a small pail or pails, a plastic shovel or other digging tool, a stick or similar shaping tool (plastic utensils are great for this!), and a spray bottle. Now get your toddler involved.

Define a square, rectangular, or round foundation pad. Have the little one dig out a deep moat around the pad while you wet, level, and tamp down the foundation. (The deeper the moat, the better, because it's cool to watch water follow the moat around the building without harming any of your work.) Have your child pack moist sand into the pail, then turn it upside down at the corner or in the middle of the foundation to create a tower. Repeat as desired or use different sized pails to create a "layer-cake" tower. To build walls, you and your buddy should mound sand and cut walls out of the mounds with the shovel. Taper any walls at the top.

Use plastic utensils or a fid to cut out steps or create details such as windows or a brick texture. Spray down the sand as you work before it dries out. When you're done, take a picture with your toddler, posing next to the sandcastle. Then, at the end of the day, leave the sandcastle but take all your implements and any garbage.

MAKE RAINY DAYS FUN

Rainy days can try a dad's patience, because a toddler will find new ways to release ample pent-up energy. Some simple, fun activities can focus your toddler and turn a day inside from trying to delightful. Start with "Color Collector." Roll colored modeling compound (like Play-Doh) into small balls. Break strands of uncooked spaghetti in half and stick one half in each ball. Line up the balls with the spaghetti pointed up. Fill a bowl with Froot Loops or similar cereal and give your toddler the task of dropping the right loop onto the spaghetti ball color. This helps your youngster practice identifying individual colors.

Have some bubble wrap left over in your shipping supplies? Use blue painter's tape to stick a strip of the packing material about 1 foot (30 cm) down a hallway. Tell your toddler it's a landing strip and that he needs to pop the bubbles so the plane can land. It's a delight-inducing, energy-burning, time-consuming exercise that can include jumping, rolling, or popping the bubbles one at a time.

Use that painter's tape and squares of colored paper to mark off a winding trail along any bare floor. Challenge your toddler to hop the entire trail—miss a square and he has to start again. The exercise increases balance and motor skills and tires the tyke out for naptime!

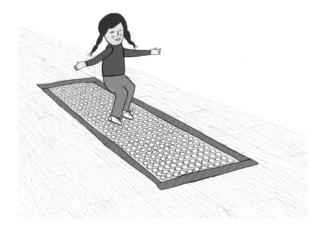

A MAGIC TRICK TO AMAZE YOUR TODDLER(S)

Always have a little something in your bag of tricks to surprise and delight your kiddo. A gang of toddlers is even better; they'll interact to figure out how you did what you just did. All you'll need to pull this one off is a scrap of paper and your hands.

Explain about Jack and Jill, two doves who were forever together. Make it a dramatic story, as you tear two fingernail-size pieces of paper. Wet them with your tongue and stick one on the middle fingernail of each hand. Introduce the pieces as Jack and Jill.

Rest your middle fingers right next to each other on the edge of a coffee table or other flat surface. Your other fingers should be pointed down. Now say, "Fly away Jack!" and quickly fling your hand over your shoulder, bringing it back down as you deftly switch fingers and set your ring finger on the edge of the table. Repeat with the opposite hand. The kids will think Jack and Jill have actually flown off. Bring them back by doing the trick in reverse.

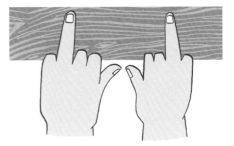

SWIM SMART WITH A TODDLER

Swim time is the time to play it boringly safe with your toddler. Luckily, even if you practice responsible water safety with the little squirt, you're both still guaranteed to have tons of fun.

Whether it's the ocean or a lazy river, any time you're around or in water with your toddler, she should never be more than arm's length from you. Any toddler even close to water—on the shore, on a pier, inside the fence surrounding a pool—should be wearing a personal floatation device. That's not water wings, a pool noodle, or an inflatable toy or raft. It's something strapped on that can keep that child afloat no matter what. Sunscreen is a must as well. Studies show people usually underapply sunscreen, so slather your youngster; she won't mind.

You can start your little one in swimming classes as young as one or two, something advocated by the Academy of American Pediatrics. You can also practice basic swim strokes and treading water as part of your child's wet fun time. Just be sure to hold onto her whatever she does in the water.

CREATE AND PLAY WITH EDIBLE FINGER PAINTS

Admit it—you still have a fondness for finger painting. It's probably one of the things you looked forward to when you thought about the toddler phase. The problem is, toddlers have a habit of sticking things in their mouths, and a lot of finger paints on the market aren't exactly palatable. So why not make your own?

It's super simple. You'll just need equal parts white flour (buy organic) and warm water. Mix the two in a bowl with a whisk, until smooth and lump free. Then divide the base into four small but finger-friendly containers (preferably disposable). Now add food coloring to each to create a set of primary colors. Or mix a bigger batch and create more colors by mixing and matching colorings. Now you can paint with the little artist and not worry about the odd mouthful. Just be sure the masterpieces are confined to kitchen and cleanable surfaces.

PLAY THE MATCH GAME

You know the value of a good education. (You should, given how much coin you throw into that college fund every month!) That's why you find games for your toddler that not only amuse him but also help develop his memory. For that, it's hard to beat the Match Game.

This version of the age-old classic switches things up a bit. Instead of buying a deck of picture cards, you'll make your own. Have your little one draw pictures of his ten favorite toys, family members, animals, or a mix. Scan and print or photocopy those pictures and cut all the images into the same-size cards.

Start with five pairs. (That's plenty challenging and, depending on the toddler's age, you may need to scale it back more.) As he becomes more proficient, add more pairs. Let the bumble see all the card faces, then turn them facedown, into a pile, and mix them up. Line them up in two or three rows. Let him turn over two to find a match. Then you go. You may be surprised at how good your toddler's memory really is (or how bad yours is!).

CRAFT CARDBOARD TUBE FUN

You're not a cheap guy, but you know as well as anyone that the best price for toys is free. Toddlers' tastes are fickle. Any toy, no matter how expensive, will quickly fall out of favor and wind up in the bottom of a donation box in a year. But you don't need store-bought toys. You redefine dad creativity, and that begins by reusing material sitting in your recycle bin right now.

Some of the most useful play-adaptable recyclables are cardboard tubes left over from paper towels and toilet paper. Although you can no doubt come up with 1,001 craft ideas for these handy items (cardboard tube monster-robot, anyone?), you can also use them for fun games that make them more than a one-time wonder.

A cardboard tube bowling set is the height of simplicity. Cut five paper towel tubes in half, paint each half white with craft paint, and add stripes at one end with red tape to make the pins. Set the pins up at the end of a hallway and let your toddler use a softball or similar to knock the pins over.

Even more fun can be had with a wall golf ball run. Use a mix of toilet paper and paper towel tubes to make a gravity-feed course for golf balls. Tape the tubes to a wall with blue painter's tape to create as complicated a course as possible. (The tape is easily removable when the time comes and won't leave any residue or marks.) Cut some tubes in half lengthwise as chutes (or cut openings as drop slots) to make the course more interesting. Once your toddler gets the idea, she'll make her own design modifications. Then drop the golf ball and see how well the course works.

You can go wild with a course like this, covering an entire wall of your toddler's bedroom. Paint the tubes or wrap them in crepe paper, punch small holes so it's easy to view the ball rolling through the tubes, or otherwise modify the tubes to delight your kiddo. Any wall course can be endlessly edited.

CRAFT A FELT LEARNING BOARD

The wise dad knows that when it comes to toddlers, almost every play activity is a chance to teach basic principles or develop skills. This simple project will translate to gobs of fun for your little one, while teaching him all about shapes and colors. Plus, it just feels cool on tiny fingers.

You'll need a large swatch of felt and several smaller pieces, all of which can be purchased from a crafts store. You can make the board just about any proportions you want, but 2' × 3' (61 × 91.4 cm) is a good, manageable size. The backer board can be a recycled cardboard box, but poster board will be more stable and secure.

To make the board, set the large piece of felt on a clean, flat surface like a table. Smooth it out and lay the backer board on top so that there is a margin of felt all around. Fold the felt over the board, working on one side at a time and overlapping at the corners as you would canvas on a frame. Secure the felt to the board with a hot glue gun, strong packing tape, or—if the board is thick enough—staples. Make sure the felt is fairly taut all the way around.

Cut a variety of shapes in different sizes, out of different colored felts. Mount the felt board on an easel or—much better—to a wall using two-sided hook-and-loop mounting strips (available at craft stores, hardware stores, or large home centers) or other hangers. Make sure, however you mount it or support, that the board is low enough for your toddler to reach.

Press the shapes onto the board. Work with your toddler to make a train of shapes or organize the felt by shape or by color. Once he becomes comfortable and engaged with the shapes, you can move onto other concepts, such as how two triangles can make a square. If your toddler falls in love with the board, you can find precut shapes—such as animals, letters, and houses—at craft stores and art supply houses. This type of board can become a teaching tool right into elementary school years.

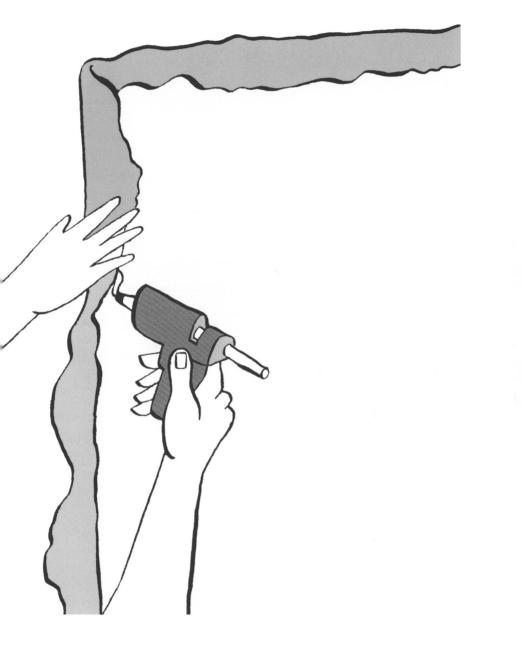

BUILD AN IMPRESSIVE CARDBOARD FORT

When it comes to impressing toddlers, imagination is half the battle. Sometimes cardboard is the other half. Use this handy building material and you can gift your tyke his first fort with little effort and just about no expense. All you need is a few boxes—the bigger, the better. If you've just moved or remodeled a kitchen and have appliance boxes leftover, you're golden. Just make sure the boxes are as thick as possible and clean.

This project starts as all successful building projects do: with a great design. Roughly sketch what you want to build. Base the structure on the phase your child is in. Just seen his first Harry Potter movie? Maybe you want a replica of an English countryside manor. Or maybe you've got a more modern child on your hands. In that case, construct the little one's very own Manhattan loft.

Next pick a site for your construction. If your toddler is lucky enough to have a large bedroom, a cardboard mansion might just fit. More likely, it needs to be put in a bonus room, garage, or even outside if you're looking at a stretch of good weather or happen to have a covered patio or deck (outside should be the last resort, though, because you're practically begging local wildlife to take up residence).

Start the actual construction with the biggest box or biggest design element. Although you can deconstruct boxes to use as walls or other elements, the fort will be the strongest if it incorporates whole boxes. Larger boxes, such as a washer or refrigerator box, are good central features—you can easily cut an access door in the front and windows on the side. As you build, enlist the help of your toddler as much as possible and include brightly colored, fun decorative elements. These can range from colored duct tape to paint, markers, or stencils (great for creating faux windows) to fabric. Scissors are handy to cut details. Once you're finished, enjoy the fact that you've just completed the world's least expensive playhouse, one your child can make all his own for endless hours of fun.

TODDLER FITNESS OBSTACLE COURSE

Buff man-dad that you are, you know better than anyone that it's never too early to get into a fitness habit. Starting your toddler down the active life path is a gift, one that keeps on giving. You win, too, as tuckered little ones sleep better and longer than kids with pent-up energy. A toddler obstacle course is an ideal way to combine fun and fitness.

Create an interesting, inexpensive, and safe course using your imagination and materials you can find around the house. Link each station with stepping "stones." These can be upside down plant pot saucers, old paint can lids, or similar objects. Set them out in a pattern that requires the toddler to leap, and include a straight line of stones to force the toddler to hop.

The stations themselves are a where you can go wild. Tape together used cardboard boxes to create a challenge tunnel (watch for staples or other sharp objects). Paint or decorate the boxes with directional arrows or other decorations. Add a balance-beam walk by securing lengths of 4 × 4 boards or similar lumber in a firmed bed of soil. Include an angle in the walk so the toddler has to turn slightly while balancing. Secure the beams to the ground so that they don't wobble underfoot.

A coordination test is a must too. Set out a saucer or large spoon and a golf ball. The toddler must pick up the golf ball on the saucer or spoon and carry it without dropping it to the drop-off bucket ten or so feet away. If he drops it, he has to come back. Increase the difficulty for older toddlers with a zigzag course of small, upside down plant pots or coffee mugs that the toddler must weave through.

Crawling's a part of any good obstacle course, which is why you should also include a jungle crawl section. Place dowels, broomsticks, or string across the top of concrete blocks; or use pool noodles staked on each end to create a hooped crawling section. There should be grass or carpet underneath so that you're toddler doesn't get too grimy. You can also add a crawl-through tunnel by linking cardboard boxes with duct tape, cutting various openings and outlets, to make a course with turns in it.

MAKE YOUR OWN MODELING DOUGH

You are not the type of man who buys something you can easily build, and that is a lesson you want your offspring to learn. Toddlers love to play with colored dough, that uniquely evocative modeling clay-like substance that is the raw material of pure imagination. It's an easy thing to make, and the making can be an opportunity to include your toddler in a crafty process.

Set up shop in the kitchen for two reasons: First the materials you need are already there. Second the process gets messy near the end, so you'll want to make sure the area and the child are easy to clean up—because that little one is going to want to play with her creation just as soon as she makes it.

There are many different recipes for homemade modeling dough. Many involve cooking the material, which will rule out the involvement of younger toddlers. That's why this recipe doesn't and is super easy for even the youngest toddler. You'll need 1½ cups (187.4 g) of white all-purpose flour, ¾ cup (219 g) of ordinary table salt, ¾ cup (177.4 ml) of lukewarm water, and different colors of food coloring. It will be helpful to have a wet dish towel on hand. A plastic tablecloth for the table will be a big plus. Set out four bowls on the table.

In a large mixing bowl, have your cooking buddy combine the flour and salt and then pour the water all over the dry ingredients. Now the fun part: You and the little one have to knead the mixture until it is the familiar consistency. If it comes out too dry, add a little water. If the mix is wet, add flour. Easy peasy. When it's the right texture, divide the dough into four roughly equal balls and pop one in each bowl. Now add a few drops of food color to each bowl and mix it into the balls until they are uniform color throughout (clean everybody's hands between colors). Transfer the balls to individual cleaned and reused yogurt containers with lids or to plastic slide-lock sandwich bags. Then clean up the kitchen and let the fun begin!

FREE A TODDLER'S HEAD STUCK IN STAIR BANNISTERS

No dad ever thinks it will happen to him; you turn your back for one second and your toddler suddenly has managed to jam his head between the bars of your stair railing or between the posts on a safety gate. Some kids even perform this trick on decorative fences. Kids—go figure.

Problem is, in defiance of logic and physics, try though you might, you cannot get the head out or pull the kid back free. It can be a panicking situation that has led to more than one call to the fire department. On that note, the secret to solving this particular riddle is to keep your cool.

Stay calm and keep your little one calm as well. The answer is exactly opposite of what you would assume. When the child is not thrashing about, turn his body so that it is lined up with the gap between the two balusters and then pull him through and out from the head side. It works because children's heads are nearly fully developed and oversized in relation to their bodies.

IDENTIFY AND TREAT PINKEYE

Sending a toddler to daycare or preschool is a recipe for sharing germs. Sooner or later, your little one is going to come home with something and, possibly—over time—everything. The trick is to know what you're dealing with and how fast or decisively you need to act.

Pinkeye (conjunctivitus) is a common ailment among school-age and pre-school-age kids. It is an infection that can be caused by a virus, bacteria, allergens, or just excessive exposure to irritants. It becomes obvious as discoloration, itching, and inflammation around and in the eye. The eye may weep water or even a white, yellow, or green discharge; and the eyelids may be crusty in the morning. The eyes can feel gritty and itchy, and the toddler may be sensitive to light.

Pinkeye calls for an immediate visit to the doctor to determine that it is, in fact, pinkeye and not something more serious. Depending on the cause of the infection, the doctor will prescribe antibiotic eye drops or ointment and/or regularly washing the eye out and using cold or warm compresses to reduce swelling and irritation. In any case, you usually can't send your little one back to daycare or preschool until the infection clears up.

PREVENT CRIB CLIMB-OUT

Well, dad, sooner or later you're very likely to come in to your toddler's room to check how naptime is progressing only to be greeted with the sight of your bumble, one leg over the top rail, making her escape. Climbing out of the crib is a fairly common occurrence among children younger than two (two to three is the age they usually move to a big kid bed, once they express the desire to).

A heartfelt "no" and your angry face are usually enough to dissuade most toddlers from trying the foolhardy move again. But if your escape artist is dead set on getting out on her own power, you may need to invest in a crib tent, which is exactly what it sounds like: a mesh screen tent that attaches to the sides of the crib, making escape nigh impossible (although that's what they said about Alcatraz).

RECOGNIZE CHICKENPOX

You're a compassionate dad; you don't want your kiddo to suffer. So you hate the idea of chickenpox. But even though there is now a vaccine for it, this disease can strike your toddler before she is vaccinated. If it does, recognizing what you're dealing with and swinging into action quickly are key to limiting the suffering.

The symptoms are usually mild and spring up rapidly ten days to three weeks after exposure. They include a mild fever and characteristic blisters on the head and torso, often spreading to the face, arms, and legs. The blisters crust over fairly quickly and then heal. The problem with outbreaks on toddlers is that they want to scratch the blisters, which can cause further infection and permanent scarring.

The first sign of chickenpox will probably be a low-grade fever and lethargy. But you quickly see a pattern of small red sores break out on the back and chest, spreading within hours.

If your toddler is uncomfortable with the fever, give her a child dose of acetaminophen (never give a child aspirin for a fever). You can alleviate some of the itching and discomfort with a lukewarm bath and mild soap or an oatmeal bath (available at pharmacies and drugstores). You can also administer a child dose of antihistamine, which may offer the dual benefit of easing itching and promoting sleep.

The other step to take is to minimize scarring by clipping your little one's fingernails (for outbreaks on the face, some parents go so far as to cover the hands with socks).

In any case, you won't need to consult a doctor unless your kid is running a fever above 102°F (38.9°C) or other symptoms worsen. However, you will need to keep her home from preschool, daycare, any play date, or contact with other children for seven days from the onset of the blisters or until they completely crust over; she's contagious for the intervening period. You can save your child the suffering of chickenpox by vaccinating at twelve to fifteen months, with a second dose of vaccine at age four to six.

TODDLER-PROOF YOUR HOME

Every year, many young children needlessly hurt themselves in homes that have not been outfitted with basic safety features. Don't let your bumble be a statistic.

Block access. Install cabinet and drawer latches and a latch catch on the toilet seat. Store toxic materials high up in both house and garage. Push chairs all the way into tables when not in use and push tabletop items to the center of the table. Store knives out of reach and cook on the back burners. Use safety gates on stairs and netting over stair-rail balusters, other handrails, and porch railings. Shorten drapery and blind cords out of reach of short people. Use safety covers on stove and TV knobs and faucets. Move houseplants out of reach and keep bathroom doors closed.

Be electrically smart. Use electrical outlet covers in every room and anchor all lamps. Secure electrical cords so that they can't be use to pull an appliance down.

Stop accidents. Use unbreakable dishware and glassware for daily use. Affix decals on any glass doors at the toddler's level. Install antiscald regulators on faucets and set the water heater below 120°F (48.9°C). Use safety straps on standing bookshelves and entertainment centers, as well as other top-heavy standing furniture. Add corner guards to sharp-edged furniture. Use door handle guards for older toddlers, as well as window stops. Remove all tablecloths.

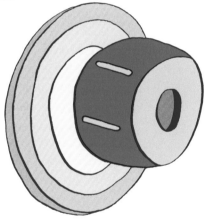

PERFORM CPR ON A TODDLER

It's the worst of all possible situations: You find your toddler unresponsive. No matter the cause, you need to swing into action.

First grab the child's shoulder and say his name loudly. If he doesn't respond, ask someone nearby to call 911 or, if you're alone, wait until you've done two rescue breaths and then call yourself.

Start with rescue breaths only if the child is not breathing. Lay him flat on his back with head tilted and chin lifted. Pinch the nose shut, seal your mouth over his, and breathe into the toddler's mouth twice, just enough to expand the chest. Check for breathing by keeping the head tilted back and putting your ear close to the mouth. If he doesn't respond to rescue breaths, start CPR.

Kneel alongside him and place the heel of your hand over his sternum and put the heel of your second hand over the first, interlacing the fingers. (Different sources recommend different hand positions: Some advise using one hand with two fingers of the other. The point is to compress the chest firmly but not damage the child's internal organs or bones.) Do thirty chest compressions, compressing the chest about 2 inches (5.1 cm) each time.

Finish with two rescue breaths. If he still doesn't respond, continue with the pattern until help arrives or the child begins breathing on his own.

REMOVE A FOREIGN OBJECT FROM YOUR TODDLER'S NOSE

Oh, those kiddos. Curious, experimental, and . . . just a little bit nutso. Sooner or later you're likely to experience the unique puzzlement of finding that your smart little child has gotten something stuck up his nose. Head-shaking as it may be, it needs to come out.

First off, if you can't see or touch the obstruction, it's cause for a visit to the doctor. If you can see it, you can remove it yourself. But this calls for abundant caution and finesse. The primary goal is not to push the object further up in the nose. That's why you're going to make one attempt; if it doesn't work, off you go to the emergency room.

Tweezers are great for large objects that aren't likely to travel any higher (a jumbo plastic brick). For smaller objects, try the "mother's kiss." Lay the toddler down with his head slightly elevated. Put your mouth over his mouth, pinch closed the unobstructed nostril, and gently blow. The air may loosen small objects that are further up the nose. If not, turn to a pro.

LOSE THE PACIFIER

Oh, man, can a pacifier be a lifesaver. A pacifier can work magic for halting any fussing in its tracks or getting a toddler to sleep. Unfortunately toddlers aren't about moderation. They like the security of a pacifier, and they like it all the time. But once your child passes his first birthday, look for opportunities to wean him off the security device. And definitely don't bump up against the second birthday, by which point a pacifier can start affecting tooth development.

Wean is the operative word here. Cold turkey leads to cranky toddlers (although some parents prefer to put up with a couple of days of misery just to get the process over with, and some experts advocate this). In any case, experts all agree that you shouldn't attempt pacifier deprivation if the toddler is adjusting with big life events, like a new daycare, a new house, or a new babysitter.

Don't go it alone. When you begin the process, make sure you inform all the caregivers at daycare or preschool, and any babysitters and relatives who spend time with the toddler. Everybody has to be clear on the policy, regardless of whether they agree with what you're doing.

Once you begin the process of weaning, institute pacifier-free periods, slowly reducing the window of use. In times when you would normally employ it—tired, cranky moments—try substitutes such as rocking; cuddling; introducing a very soft, tactile stuffed toy; or simply soothing the child with quiet reassurances.

When you're ready to go full stop, pretend to lose the pacifier and ask your child to help you find it. Once neither of you can locate it, reassure him that you'll look for it later and move on. This is an especially good strategy for nap or bedtime, when the child is already primed to go to sleep. You can also be more aboveboard about it and introduce a pacifier fairy much like a tooth fairy—each pacifier given to "the fairy" results in a present—or use "the stick" rather than the carrot and coat the pacifier with lemon juice or vinegar.

BEAT A TEMPER TANTRUM

As your tyke grows into her own person and experiments with independence and free will, there will be frustration. As patience-testing as any tantrum can be, there are a many strategies that will help you navigate the storm back to happier and calmer waters.

Always remember who the adult is. The tantrum itself is a result of frustration at lack of control over being made to do something or being prevented from doing something. You hold all the cards. A tantrum is a very limited event in the span of a day. Communicate with your child quietly, without getting mad or showing frustration. Yeah, it's easier said than done, but it will prove a much more effective attitude in the long run (and you avoid that unique shame and regret that comes from yelling at a toddler).

Your reaction should take place and circumstance into account. At home, it may be wisest to let the tantrum burn itself out while you keep a watchful eye that the child doesn't act out inappropriately or hurt herself. In a store or other public place, it makes more sense—and is often more considerate—to remove the toddler to a more private setting such as your car or a bathroom for the duration of the tantrum. Just don't do it angrily.

Humor can defuse less strident tantrums. A funny face or even a fake laugh can, in the right moment, take all the steam out of a tantrum. Also give a brief moment of thought if you can easily accommodate the cause of the tantrum without it being bribery—for instance, allowing a third toy on a car trip rather than the two you specified.

The boundary for any tantrum should be if the toddler is at risk of hurting herself or someone else or destroying something. Smashing, hitting, and biting are all tantrum actions that call for a time-out and a stern talking to. In any case, after the tantrum has played out, reassure the bumble that you love her. The child will forget about the outburst and move on, and so should you.

STOP NOSE PICKING

Let's face it: kids are gross. When it comes to nose picking, you can dial back the grossness. Start with this: There is usually a reason for the behavior—removing something that has collected there.

That's why the first order of business is addressing any allergies that your toddler might be experiencing. Make sure the child is properly hydrated, because dehydration and dry air can both lead to buildup in the nostrils. When you catch the behavior in progress, use a tissue to clear the nostrils and make sure your toddler knows how to use one and has one on him at all times. If nose picking has become habitual, you can put an adhesive bandage on the guilty finger, which will often stop the bad habit in its tracks.

Regardless of how successful you are in curbing the behavior, make sure your little one's fingernails are trimmed to avoid cutting or injuring sensitive nasal membranes.

MAKE TUB TIME HAPPY TIME

Tub time can be a two-way challenge when dealing with a toddler. It can be a bit of a battle getting him or her into the tub to start with, and some kids are equally resistant to getting out. A few simple strategies can ease the way for parent and toddler.

Toys equal fun, so make sure you have a good supply of bath toys. These don't have to be store-bought toys. Colorful funnels, plastic measuring cups, and other seemingly mundane plastic utensils can be conduits for a toddler's imagination. But keep yourself sane by coming up with a way to store floatable toys. A net holder with suction cups can be ideal, or even a small plastic trunk or bucket can serve the purpose. Whatever the storage, the rule is that bath toys remain in the bathroom.

Another hard-and-fast rule is sitting. Toddlers may decide they want to stand, but that's an accident waiting to happen. That's why any toddler bath—no matter how independent the toddler—requires complete adult supervision. You also want to make sure that washing happens in the tub. If the kiddo won't do it himself, you'll need to use a washcloth to clean top to bottom. Lastly, limit a bath to 15 minutes tops. Any longer and you risk drying out your bumble's skin.

DISCIPLINE YOUR TODDLER

Imposing discipline is worst part of being a father, but it's also essential if your toddler is going to grow up to a responsible, social, well-adjusted adult.

Be alert to trouble times. Transitioning from a pleasurable activity to a required-but-less pleasurable activity can be a trigger for acting out. Give plenty of warning that lunch is coming up and the toy car will have to be parked.

Know what matters. Maybe butt bouncing on an overstuffed couch isn't such a crime. Discipline is a matter of degrees. If it isn't hurting him or the house, and it's just you in a rush, perhaps you want to slow down and let your toddler be a toddler.

Be firm and be direct. Why are you explaining your reasoning? Something's bad, it's bad. You say so. So, "No," is enough. A toddler may not have the language skills to even understand an explanation. He needs to know that when you say no, that simply means "no."

Keep your cool. This is the cardinal rule. Discipline goes wrong when you get angry and want to show that kid who's boss. You'll know you're headed off the rails when you grab your little one, feel yourself getting angry, or your volume climbs. Sometimes it's wiser to walk away. On the same note, no hitting. The main lesson violence teaches? That violence is a way to resolve problems.

Short-circuit attention getting. The moment you're in the middle of a complicated recipe or painting a wall, that's when your toddler most desires your attention. Think ahead and preoccupy the little one when you need to get something done.

Use enlightened language. Straight from child psychologists, you can head off a lot of self-esteem issues simply by how you phrase things. It's never "You are being bad" but "Dumping your milk on the carpet is bad." It can have a big impact.

Start time-outs early. You may think that the simple time-out is a device for older kids, but toddlers can be put in time-out just as easily. And the impact of that simple punishment can be profound.

Always wind up in a good place. Any discipline needs to be followed by expressions of support. As soon as reasonable, assure that little troublemaker that you still love and, just as important, like him.

STOP A TODDLER FROM BITING

It's not like you have a mini Dracula in your home; lots of toddlers bite for a variety of reasons. The key is to nip the behavior in the bud at first sight, before it turns into a problem.

Biting can be a response to frustration or anger, a way of acting for a little person who doesn't have a wide vocabulary or other tools for dealing with those feelings. But those are far from the only causes of toddler biting. Sometimes it can be an attempt to relieve teething pain, a way to give notice when the toddler is very hungry or overtired, or just something the toddler is testing out as he explores the boundaries of his world.

Whatever the cause, it's not acceptable behavior. The best offense in this case is a good defense. Start with keeping that youngster on a very regular schedule, to limit fatigue, irritation, and other conditions that can lead to biting. Give a teething toddler a cold teething ring or frozen wet washcloth to alleviate some of the discomfort.

But sometimes, there's no predicting or heading off an attack of the chompers. In that case, the first order of business is ensuring that the victim is tended to and gets any first aid or care necessary. Then kneel down and address the biter eye to eye. Be direct with a statement like, "No, we don't bite." Be firm but not angry and don't shout.

You can take preventative measures after the event, by thinking about what might have triggered the outburst. Eliminating triggers can go a long way toward preventing a single biting incident from turning into a bad habit. Coach your little one repeatedly to use words when faced with frustration. You should also reinforce any positive conflict resolutions when they happen, giving the toddler a reason to continue those behaviors.

Whatever you do, don't hit a biter and don't buy into the common misconception that biting a biter will stop the behavior. You'll simply be sending the message that biting is a legitimate recourse in certain circumstances.

TOILET TRAIN TROUBLE-FREE

You're a good dad, but who could blame you for wanting to get out from under diaper duty? That's why toilet training isn't just a profound stage for the toddler; it's a major hallmark for parents as well. Unfortunately you won't necessarily have as much say in the decision as you might like. That's because although children as young as one may be ready to potty train, some toddlers may not be totally ready until they're bumping up against their third birthdays. The vast majority will fall in the middle, being ready for toilet training between 18 and 24 months.

Before any toddler can start toilet training, she has to be able to hold her bladder for up to 2 hours, be mobile enough to get on and off a child-size toilet by herself, clearly communicate when she needs to use the bathroom and, perhaps most important, want to use the toilet rather than a diaper. That last one is key if you don't want a long, pitched battle on your hands.

When all signs point to "yes," set up for success with a toilet-training seat for the toilet or, better yet, a training potty sized for the youngster. Get your toddler accustomed to the toilet by having her sit on it regularly, preferably every couple of hours. Make sure you keep your antenna up for when your little one shows signs that she has to go. Get her to the bathroom as quickly as possible to head off using the diaper and get her used to linking the need with the facilities.

If you're the proud dad of girl child, reinforce along the way the need for good hygiene to avoid infections (wiping from front to back when done). And never let your child forget to wash his or her hands immediately after going to the bathroom.

As soon as reasonable (a day of dry diapers), transition your toddler out of diapers and into training underwear. It shows the child that she's making progress and she will probably be as happy as you are to be done with diapers.

DEAL WITH A PACK OF TODDLERS

Sooner or later, you're going to discover why preschool teachers are worth twice whatever they get paid. Whether it's a group play date, a birthday party, or just a child-focused gathering, a pack of toddlers is a force of nature that will take you to the limits of your awareness and patience.

The rule of thumb is to limit group size for toddlers younger than three to six kids per attentive adult. That means for larger gangs, you'll need to rope in another adult. Maintaining close supervision means limiting the group to a large room or constricted outdoor space. Toddlers are fast, and if one makes it to an adjacent room or goes missing, your attention will be diverted from supervising the group. The space should be toddler-proofed and entirely safe so you don't have to worry about kids hurting themselves.

A group activity is key. When you direct what everybody is doing, you ensure they aren't doing something else—like stress-testing your TV remote. Simple games such as tag or duck, duck, goose can be wonderful ways to keep everyone involved. Even if you've set up activities, though, be on the lookout for conflicts and break up any spats immediately. Keep in mind that reading to toddlers can be a great group activity if the book is short and simple. This is especially true if you're willing to take on the characters in the book and adopt dramatic voices and facial expressions. Toddlers will gladly devote their attention to something completely over the top. As an alternative, you can play age-appropriate music and have the group dance and sing along. Just be sure that you have earplugs on hand for yourself.

If you're willing to go the extra mile, a simple meal (if the group is gathering around lunchtime) will be just as good as a group activity at clustering the little ones around a common purpose.

Plan a schedule of activities and a time to break up the group. Even the most well-behaved group of toddlers will eventually hit the wall and become tired, hungry, irritable, and ready to go home and have some downtime.

3

Don't forget to
enjoy this
prehormonal
phase of life.

CHAPTER 3

The Single-Digit Challenge

Congratulations! You've made it through the harried toddler stage. Give yourself and your long-suffering better half a pat on the back. Now take a deep breath and get ready for a whole new level of fun with an increasingly independent little person full of a thirst for discovery and . . . hell-bent on having his or her own way.

That's really the double-edged sword of ages three to ten—your child will need less and less moment-to-moment care and oversight, but he or she will also be forging personal opinions and making decisions on which of your rules to follow and which can be bent to the point of breaking. You'll need to know when to draw the line and when to allow a certain amount of latitude in service of personal growth.

This is a time of radical change in any child's life, marked most dramatically by the start of elementary school. That's where you'll find out how smart your child is and possibly rediscover the gaps in your own education. Make no mistake, though, this can be a fascinating time. The young mind is a sponge, and your role as dad can help that sponge stay absorbent. School may be where your little one gets an education, but you can offer help when your budding student needs it. More important, with a little effort you can bring classroom lessons to life, making learning more fun, exciting, and engaging.

Keep in mind that life isn't all just learning. That's why many topics in this chapter are dedicated to the sheer fun you can have with your kiddo. Crafts, games, and holidays can all can be enjoyed to the hilt while you're still a hero and more important than any of your youngster's friends. The single digits are where some of the most powerful memories are made, and fun should a part of most of them.

Don't worry if you don't have all the answers as your kid develops by leaps and bounds; you just need to have the right ones. If your child is going to grow into a confident, successful, independent person, he or she is going to need your support and guidance—even when acting like the opposite. So be present and don't forget to enjoy this prehormonal phase of life; it's the stuff of which scrapbooks are filled.

ENCOURAGE A YOUNG READER

You're a worldly guy. That's why you know that the world opens up to a reader. The best way to expand a young brain is to get it reading. Thank goodness there are lots of ways to do that.

Make it a nightly habit. Reading to your child nightly from toddlerhood until she can read herself is a wonderful way to get any kid into the idea reading as a part of life. Plus it's a great way to slow things down and bond with the bumble.

Visit the library and bookstore. Even before she starts reading on her own, it pays to introduce your little one to the treasure of the local library. You reinforce the idea that there is a more authoritative resource than the internet. Create an early love of bookstores by making a trip to one as a reward for certain achievements or accomplishments.

Integrate books. Make books a part of home life and the young reader gets used to having them around and accessible at all time. Don't be afraid to add a bookshelf to every room, including your child's.

Set an example. The more your child sees you taking time out of your day—perhaps as a substitute to TV—to just read by choice, the more she'll understand that it's a desirable as well as useful activity.

Read beyond books. Books, magazines, and newspapers aren't the only materials that young readers can use to hone their skills. Playing games that require reading cards can be a great way for a child to practice reading and word pronunciation.

Recognize problems. Experts tells us that one in five young students will wrestle with some educational disability, and many of those—such as dyslexia—will involve reading and comprehension skills. Keep an eye out for signs that your youngster is struggling with reading and address them aggressively and without stigma.

Exploit technology. Reading is one of the best uses for the many screens in a youngster's life, and an e-reader can be a great replacement for a portable game device or other electronics.

BUILD GOOD STUDY HABITS

It may seem like a long way off, but you're probably already saving for your kid's college ambitions. Along with money, your future scholar is also going to need some educational discipline. Instilling that doesn't cost you a thing and could be more important, in the long run, than any amount of money. Good study habits are just that—habits. Build them early and they'll serve your child for life.

Make homework a priority. Study and homework should be a regularly scheduled occurrence. Even when you grade-schooler is just starting out, setting a small amount of time aside each day to at least review school lessons and look ahead at what comes next can be invaluable. If you look at it like you would brushing teeth, it becomes a normal part of routine and it is far less likely that your offspring will put off school assignments in the future.

Do your part. By the time kids reach high school, they should be entirely independent students. But in the primary grades, they usually need some help getting squared away. Squared away is your middle name, so jump right in, Dad. Help your young student prioritize workload, set goals, and organize himself. Teach him to tackle the hardest assignments first, when the mind is the freshest.

Review homework assignments. Going over the homework your grade-schooler brings home serves two goals: It helps keep you in the know about where he is in his studies and what's going on at school, and it gives you a chance to help your kid focus and organize whatever he needs to do to complete the assignment.

Identify resources. At one point or another, every student needs some help. But unless the particular individual is very outspoken and confident, he's unlikely to ask for it. Be aware of how much your kiddo is struggling with any given subject. When things get difficult, it may be worth a call to the teacher to advocate for more one-on-one attention; or it may be a case where bringing in a tutor can keep your child stay in the flow.

INTRODUCE NIGHTLY DINNER-TABLE RECAPS

Where kids are concerned, getting the complete 411 can be a bit of a struggle. The secret? An age-old family ritual—the sit-down dinner. Getting kids to the table means imposing a regular dinnertime and place. No more than one exception a week.

Prompt the discussion with specific rather than general questions. "Any new math lessons today?" rather than "What happened in school today?" You can be off the wall and goofy to cut through kids' natural defenses. But once you get them talking, let them go. Often they will keep talking after the question is answered, because it has spurred other memories.

When there is little school news, don't hesitate to turn to news stories, but frame them as teachable lessons or departure points for debate. Be careful how you react once the faucet of info is opened. Let the dinner table be a largely judgment-free zone or your young ones will quickly learn that it's in their best interests to clam up.

MAKE WRITING ENJOYABLE

Written communications are some of the most powerful and quickly becoming a lost art form. But that doesn't have to be the case with your youngster. You can instill a love of writing in your child with just a little one-on-one time.

Although good writing translates to electronic media, it's wise to get your tyke accustomed to writing longhand. Spell-check features are far from perfect, and your child should learn proper spelling, punctuation, and grammar.

Have your kiddo write a letter to his favorite musician or movie star. Or, even nicer, to a friend or relative who lives far away. Your child will undoubtedly find the process of writing a letter, putting it on an envelope, and adding a stamp both novel and kind of fun. Of course, writing doesn't need to be long form or conventional. Engage the early reader while improving dialog skills by buying comic book blank pages. These are available widely at online retailers and in larger brick-and-mortar craft outlets. Even if your little one doesn't have art skills, he can always cut and paste characters from magazines, adding the words himself.

IDENTIFY AND DEAL WITH
LEARNING DISABILITIES

Finding out your precious little one has a learning disorder is like a punch to the gut. A disorder that seems to come out of the blue drives home the fact that you don't have as much control as you would like. But ignoring a problem is even worse for your child.

Before you swing into action, the problem needs to be detected. Fortunately most teachers, including many preschool teachers, are trained in spotting learning disabilities early on. There are a lot of different cognitive disorders, but general clues can point to an overall problem. These include difficulty memorizing even small amounts of information; inability to follow instructions or see a task all the way through; difficulty staying focused, coupled with a short attention span; outbursts with no apparent cause or pattern; working very slowly through school assignments or in-class projects; and a tendency to always be behind the level and amount of work the rest of the class is doing.

There are even earlier indicators. If your toddler was especially late to walk, talk, or was poor at socializing with others, those may have been signs.

It's terrible to feel that you're helpless to help the one you love most in the world, on the back of a learning disorder diagnosis. But you're not. Not by a long shot. Most important, be your child's advocate. Make sure he has the best teaching available in your school system. Check out local, county, and state resources and take advantage of them. It may mean a regular in-house tutor. It may mean spending money on after-school programs to help slower kids catch up. It may mean a lot of things, but getting it right can mean the difference between a future of opportunity or one of frustrating struggle for your child.

It's important to destigmatize the disability. Kids know when they're different from other kids, and it's not pleasant. Go out of your way to find understanding playmates. And communicate to your kiddo that it's simply a challenge you'll overcome together. Love him unconditionally and remember that he's dealing with a life-affecting problem that will impact his mood and outlook. Make sure he knows he has your support.

CRAFT A GEOGRAPHY RELIEF MAP
WITH THE KIDDO

You know that somewhere down inside you have an artist waiting to get out. Well here's a project that can help your tyke with his geography lessons while expressing both child's and father's artistic leanings.

Tangible maps with texture, color, and a three-dimensional shape are not only alluring but are better teaching tools than boring two-dimensional versions. This project offers the opportunity for your young student to dive in and create a realistic terrain with little help.

The map is crafted with a malleable salt dough (that can be useful for other home craft projects as well). You can use the dough to re-create continents, individual states, the entire United States, or just a small snapshot of geological features like peninsulas, islands, inlets, and more. Using the dough for school projects is limited only by assignments and imagination.

First find a representation outlining the area you're looking to create; trace it. Transfer the traced shape to a cardboard or poster board base. Download or look up a topographical map of the same area for reference. Next mix the salt dough. Combine 4 cups (499.7 g) of all-purpose flour, 2 cups (583.9 g) of table salt, 2 cups (473.2 ml) of lukewarm water, and 2 tablespoons (31.1 g) of cream of tartar. (These amounts will create a sizable continent map, with several different elevations and mountains.) Mix the ingredients by hand until combined.

Have your early learner spread an even base of the dough inside the outline for the shape. Now consult the topographical map and begin building up the different elevations. Your child should work as fast as possible (no breaks). He will probably need help in interpreting topographical features. Once he is satisfied with the map, let it dry. This may take a day or two.

Time to paint? Have your kiddo pick a different color for each feature—water, mountains, plains, and valleys. Have him include a key on the board to explain what each color denotes. Kids can use markers to make borders, further define specific areas, or label a given feature. The finished project will no doubt earn an "A" but, more important, will also be a great bonding exercise.

ILLUSTRATE MONEY BASICS FOR KIDS

Drive home the lessons of this project by working with your kiddo on it. It's an easy piece of crafting to complete and won't take much time. It will, however, require you invest $1.41. Well, that and the cost of some poster board.

You'll be making a chart of money equivalencies. Create five columns starting from one short edge of the poster board, working across to the other edge. Tape a dollar bill along the left edge. Even with the top of the bill, tape down a quarter, dime, nickel, and penny in that order, as column headings. Leave more room for each column as you work across to the pennies.

Now have your budding banker trace the shapes for four quarters, ten dimes, twenty nickels, and one hundred pennies under their respective headings. Explain to your child how smaller amounts can add up to larger amounts and have her color one of the quarters and then color the number of pennies that correspond to the quarter in the same color. Have her do the same for a dime and nickel.

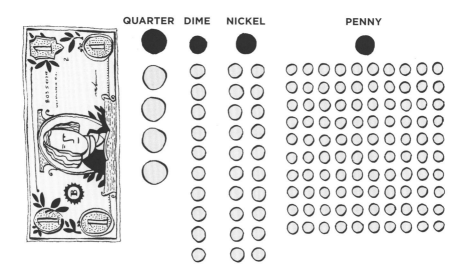

TEACH THROUGH A TELESCOPE

The easiest way to be a parent advocate for learning is to build classroom lessons into super fun activities. You'll make discovery more enjoyable for the little one and for yourself. A bonding night spent stargazing is one of the best ways to share the experience of science with your child, diving into basic astronomy, physics, and beyond.

Decode the night sky with your young astronomer by learning constellations together. You'll find many free, simple constellation star charts for the Northern Hemisphere online. Just download one and bring it outside with a small flashlight on a clear night.

Once your kiddo becomes familiar with the night sky's pattern of stars, turn to the celestial bodies. The obvious candidate—and the one that can be seen easily through even an inexpensive beginner telescope—is the moon. Always come loaded with fascinating facts and figures, like the distance from the Earth to the moon (250,000 miles [402,336 km], or roughly 1.3 million American football fields end to end). You can also purchase a moon guide from any reputable source to explore the moon's features with your grade-schooler.

MAKE YOUR OWN MOTION LAMP

Time to take a trip back to your black-lit '70s childhood bedroom! Help your kid make a motion lamp at home and you're not only taking a nostalgic walk in the past; you're doing a science experiment that will teach the youngster a bit about fluid dynamics. So get learning!

Secure a one-liter soda bottle and clean it thoroughly. Now help your kiddo pour in about 1 cup (236.6 ml) of cold water. Work with him to carefully fill up the bottle nearly to the top with vegetable oil. Add eight to twelve drops of food coloring, using your child's favorite color. Wait for the contents to settle and separate completely (the food coloring will filter through the oil and disperse in the water at the bottom of the bottle).

Now give your little scientist half of a seltzer tablet (such as Alka-Seltzer), and let him drop it in. Away we go to the blob show we call a motion lamp. You can put the bottle on top of a smartphone with its light turned on to heighten the effect, or have the little one hold a flashlight under the bottle with the lights in the room turned off. You can even use a simple battery-operated puck light as a light pedestal.

Time to teach! Ask your child why the water and oil stays separate (different molecular structure means oils want to bond with oils and repel water—*hydrophobic*—and water wants to bond with water and repel oil—*hydrophilic*) and why he thinks the water blobs rise (the CO_2 produced by the seltzer tablet is lighter than either the water or oil, so it rises but is activated by the water, which is captured by bubbles of the gas). Discuss with the kiddo the relative weights of liquids and why one would sit below another (because it's heavier, duh). You can also use this as a leaping-off point to try other experiments, such as combining other liquids in a bottle to determine their weights (e.g., heavy cream and rubbing alcohol).

The lamp can be used repeatedly, just by dropping in another half of a seltzer tablet!

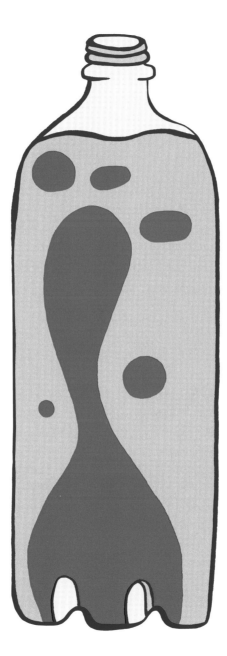

STOP YOUR CHILD FROM WETTING THE BED

It's one of the more frustrating situations of parenthood: You wake up bleary eyed at 3 a.m. because your child is crying or standing sheepishly at your bedside. You struggle out of bed, get the little one calmed down, and start in on the process of getting him into new, dry pajamas and stripping wet linens from the bed. By the time you slip back under the covers, you're silently praying that you don't get another rude wake-up call at 5 a.m.

Experts define bed-wetting as any nocturnal, involuntary urination while asleep, past the age of five. But frankly, if you're nearly-four-year-old is doing it, it's officially bed-wetting to you. Although rarely caused by an underlying medical issue, it should be mentioned to your pediatrician. More often than not, the cause is simple—ranging from milk allergies to a slow-maturing bladder. And there are some strategies to head off the problem.

Limit suspect foods and drink. Certain foods—including any that contain caffeine, such as sodas or hot chocolate—can irritate the bladder and are best avoided. Cut out anything with red dye or other food colorings in it, citrus, or artificial sweeteners. More rarely, milk allergies can lead to bed-wetting. If this is the case, eliminate dairy from the child's diet.

Regulate fluid intake. Make sure your child drinks lots of fluids during the day to stay hydrated—but taper off in the afternoon and try to eliminate any fluids within a couple hours of bedtime.

Enforce a bathroom schedule. Check in with your little one at regular, scheduled intervals to make sure he's urinating. One of the breaks should be right before bedtime every night.

Never punish; often reward. Trust this: No child wants to wet his bed. It's as unpleasant for him as it is for you. Always keep in mind that this is a stage and your child *will* stop wetting the bed; reward even small steps toward that end and support your child when he's feeling bad about wetting the bed.

Some parents are advised to wake a child up in the middle of the night for a bathroom break. This isn't a good idea, because it's not going to short-circuit the underlying cause.

BUILD SELF-CONFIDENCE

A strong, positive, enduring sense of self is one of the most wonderful gifts you can hand down to your offspring.

Give unconditional love. Every parent gets frustrated, occasionally angry, and tired. Parents are only human. But it's worth making these three words your motto, because they let your child know that he's always supported.

Support safe risk-taking and adventure. Your child is going to attempt some risky things in the world, and sooner or later you're going to have to let him push his limits. Keep him safe from physical harm, but let him explore his capabilities.

Reject comparison. Theodore Roosevelt said, "Comparison is the thief of joy." Make sure your child isn't measuring himself against anyone else.

Constantly encourage. Encouragement isn't the same as praise. Praise can be misguided and is often given falsely or for something that doesn't deserve praise. Encouragement is support, no matter what the child does or how well.

DISCIPLINE WITHOUT SPANKING

Imposing violence on a child only legitimizes violence as an option. There are plenty of alternative strategies to punish an errant child.

Give a time-out. This classic can be done almost anywhere. Just put the child in isolation for a short time to "think about what he's done."

Suspend privileges. You can take away screen time, lock up toys, or postpone pleasurable activities as a powerful way to get across the message that misbehavior won't be tolerated.

Link cause and effect. Did your kiddo forget once again to pick up his toy cars and now you've got a toy embedded in your foot? No more toy cars for a week.

Reward the good. Reinforce positive behavior to make it more desirable. Surprise a child with a toy for cleaning up his room without being asked.

COMBATTING HEAD LICE

Thank goodness you're the type of manly dad who doesn't get grossed out by much. Because if your kid is one of the millions each year that comes home from school with head lice, that resolve is going to be tested. These disgusting little insects are repulsive but easy to eliminate. The key is to catch them early and eradicate them fully.

Before anybody falls victim to the stigma of head lice, be clear that the vermin don't discriminate. Anyone can get lice, and your head, hair, or body doesn't need to be dirty. In fact, you and your house could be squeaky clean, and lice would be quite happy there. The good news is that even though they may be one of the grossest problems you'll come across with your youngster, head lice don't carry disease.

The first step in combatting these pests is detecting them. Sit your little one on a chair under bright direct light and use a comb to part the hair on the top of the head. Carefully inspect the scalp and the base of the hair shafts. Adult lice may be hard to detect because they hate light and can move fairly quickly. If you see one, it will be dirty beige to tan and about the size of a piece of dandruff. You're more likely to find lice eggs, which are called nits. They are attached to the bottom of hair follicles. Continue parting the hair and looking closely.

You can also use the "comb out" method by wetting your child's hair and then combing every section of hair with a fine-tooth comb. After each stroke, wipe the comb's tines on a clean, wet paper towel or smooth black cloth. Any nits or lice should be obvious.

Although there are prescription medications for lice, the vast majority of cases can easily be remedied with over-the-counter formulas. Follow the directions on the label to the letter to ensure success. It will involve using a special shampoo for the child's hair (and anyone else on in the house who has picked up the critters), as well as washing clothing, hats, and bed linens with a special soap.

Lice Egg

LIBERTY

D

2019

Adult Lice

TRAINING A CHILD FOR STRANGER DANGER

Unfortunately you must eventually send your little one out into the world to get where she needs to go. Sooner or later, she's going to make that trip alone, and that's why you need to train her to spot and avoid the rare individual looking to do a child harm.

First maintain perspective. Child abductions are thankfully rare, and children are statistically more likely to be mistreated by someone they know. That's why today's experts suggest you make your child aware beyond strangers (in fact, many childcare and safety pros recommend against even using that word). The phrase many use is *tricky people* or people who might try to trick the kid.

This is about striking a balance because you want your child to be courteous without getting into the ice cream truck with the weird ice cream guy. Be very careful about the language you choose to communicate that this is a serious topic, without scaring your youngster.

Set out the definite rules. Never take anything—the offer of a puppy, candy, ice cream—offered by an adult the child doesn't know. Never get into a vehicle with an unknown adult and, if anyone wants her to do that, she should run in the opposite direction the vehicle is traveling. Tell your child to trust her "inside feelings" (instincts). If an adult seems off, she should assume the adult is. Let your child know that it's okay at any time to seek help from an adult they know or from someone in uniform such as a police officer, crossing guard, or a cashier in a store. She can also turn to a mom with kids. Screaming and raising a fuss (even destroying property) is okay if an adult is trying to forcibly take her somewhere against her will.

You can help your child be prepared by setting up a code word, so that if you need someone to pick up your child after school, or post-birthday party, that person can use the code word to assure the child that the adult is safe. Limit personalizing clothing, accessories, or backpacks; predators can use a first name as valuable info to strike up a rapport with an intended target.

DEAL WITH A CHILD'S WEIGHT PROBLEM

Being a good dad means making some hard calls. You'd never want to body shame your kiddo, but with one in five adolescents in the United States crossing the line into obesity, it's important to make sure your child is a healthy weight. The first line of defense is to know what a healthy weight is.

To be clear, some huskiness may just be a stage, as your little one prepares for a growth spurt. But if you child is carrying a high body mass index (a BMI of 24 or above—ask the pediatrician), it may behoove you to take steps so that weight issues don't become a schoolyard target or a lifelong problem.

The best thing you can do, according to most child development experts, is to model good nutritional and physical fitness habits. If you eat healthy and maintain a reasonable body weight, chances are your offspring will too. That means limiting snacks, sugary drinks (including many high-fructose fruit juices), desserts, and fatty or processed foods. Focus on vegetables and turn to lean protein sources (e.g., chicken breast instead of hamburgers). You have to balance nutrition and pleasure and make an effort to cook meals that appeal to the child and will fill him up: whole-grain pastas, high-fiber fruits, and protein-packed sides like hummus.

Fast-food meals should be a rarity, and no matter where the meal comes from, limit portion sizes. Keep in mind that before the age of fourteen, a child doesn't need more than 1,800 calories a day—and possibly significantly fewer if the calories are high quality, such as complex carbohydrates and fresh fruits, vegetables, and greens.

The other part of the equation is physical activity. Children should engage in at least one hour (and preferably more) of vigorous physical activity a day. The easiest way to encourage that is to get your children playing—sports, outdoor games, or just generalized play. You can help yourself out by limiting screen time each day to a modest amount (no more than an hour of viewing anything other than schoolwork on a computer). This will help your child in another factor of healthy weight: a good night's sleep.

TEACH YOUR KID TO THROW A BASEBALL

The great thing about baseball for young athletes is that it is unlike other sports that may exclude your little one based on physical attributes. Let's face it—if your girl or boy doesn't run fast and have a lot of power, he or she is not going to play football. And if junior inherited grandpa's shortness? Basketball's probably not going to be his strong suit. But baseball is equal opportunity. A smaller, less talented player can compete just by perfecting control, fine motor skills, and basic mechanics. And the best place for kids to distinguish themselves is on the mound. Pitching rewards consistency and repetition; learn the basics and any kid can pitch well.

Be your little athlete's first, best coach. Go all the way back to basics, to break down throwing a baseball into its fundamental components, and you give your kiddo a foundation he can build on for the rest of his athletic career.

The key to good pitching mechanics is control. Teach your youngster to move at his or her own pace, slowly and steadily. Be deliberate, repeat the movement exactly each time, and the results will come.

❶ **Assume the "T" position.** This is arms out level with the shoulders, legs hip distance apart. The player should be sideways to the target, with the glove pointing at the target.

❷ **Cock and begin step.** The player breaks the level of the back arm, bringing the ball up so that the back arm forms an "L." At the same time, the player lifts the front foot, pointing the toes at the target.

❸ **Step through and throw.** While landing on the front foot, the player simultaneously pulls the front elbow into the body (the victory pump—as if the player is saying, "Yes, I won") and throws along the plane of the body toward the target. Players' eyes should always remain on the target.

HAVE FUN AND STAY FIT WITH
YOUR YOUNGSTER

The key to making fitness a family habit is integrating exercise into everyday fun activities. Shoot for at least sixty minutes of activity a day. Sports are an easy way to do that, and the best are easily adapted to one-on-one action that don't require too much gear: baseball, soccer, or basketball. Although a game of catch is more a bonding exercise than an exercise, soccer drills and a one-on-one game of basketball can raise and sustain a beneficial heart rate.

Classics such as tag or—if you have pool—Marco Polo, help get everyone moving and can bring out your inner child. Don't discount the benefits of a brisk long walk. An after-dinner or pre-bed constitutional can be a heart-healthy way to engage your youngster in discussion as well as exercise. You can also add a socially responsible spin to it and sign you and your child up for charity walks.

Lastly, a good hour of yard work or other chores can be an excellent workout. Make chores more appealing with a reward or a competition (I can finish raking my side of the lawn before you finish yours).

HELP YOUR CHILD DEAL WITH BULLIES

A child's school years can be a cruel world. Depending on the circumstances, there's a fairly good chance your kiddo will encounter a bully at some point during her primary school years. Studies suggest that the percentage of students who experience in-person bullying (as opposed to cyberbullying, which is less prevalent) is somewhere around 35 percent. More than half of kids being bullied don't feel comfortable telling an adult, often because they are embarrassed or ashamed about the situation.

That means determining if your kid is a victim is the first hurdle. Bullied children often act differently than normal. They may seem more anxious and experience poor sleep. They may also eat less than they normally do. In cases of physical bullying, your little one may often have unexplained bruises, contusions, or other small injuries; ripped or destroyed clothing; lost books; or missing accessories and money.

If you suspect your child is being bullied, have a healthy conversation. Be as supportive as possible. Explain that you're happy she could talk it about and that you'll help her find a solution. Focus on solutions and on the child, not on yourself. Don't show anger. Listen, coax out all the details, and emphasize that the bully is the one in the wrong.

Reach out to the principal, vice principal, teachers, counselors, and other authority figures who should be made aware of the problem. Although it can be tempting to coach your child to fight back, this is a risky strategy and one most experts advise against. Violence or confrontation can escalate a bullying situation.

Child-development pros counsel taking power away from the bully. Tell your child to buddy up with friends when at school. Bullies want to create fear or provoke a reaction, so a poker face can be your child's best friend. If your kid simply works on showing no emotion and walking away, she'll be sapping the bully's power. Obviously this may not be an option in the case of physical bullying. If the incident involved threats, intimidation, or actual physical violence, tell your child to remain calm, and report the incident immediately to an authority figure.

MAKE A HIDDEN VEGGIE SMOOTHIE

No, you should never deceive your child . . . unless it's for a good purpose. Helping that little one eat healthy qualifies as a good purpose. Smoothies are a quick and easy, nutrition-packed meal or snack that offers a way to get vegetable-adverse kids to eat their greens (and reds, oranges, or purples).

The key to making smoothies that your kiddo will love is to limit the number of ingredients. The urge with smoothies is to throw in everything you can but instead, let one pleasant flavor dominate. For instance, a small amount of kale and perhaps a couple chunks of beet add nutrition to a basic purple blueberry smoothie. You'll do best with sweeter fruits and vegetables such as carrots, beets, berries, and bananas.

Keep in mind that texture is as important as flavor. Chunky smoothies are smoothies that children will ignore. Use a significant amount of base—soy milk, almond milk, plain milk, or yogurt—and avoid chalky ingredients like protein powder. Blend the smoothie completely for a perfectly smooth drink. This may take a couple of minutes on high. Lastly, fun colors such as blue, red, or orange are going to be much more attractive to children than a deep green smoothie.

NURTURE MUSICAL APPRECIATION AND ABILITY

Many a potential musical prodigy has been sacrificed on the altar of a parent's failed ambitions. Music can be a lifelong love and a wonderful way to round out a child's personality, but few kids are going to stick with a musical instrument that seems like more work than fun.

Start early by singing to your infant or playing music (live or recorded) for the bumble. Expose any child to a range of music. She doesn't have to like everything, but kids start to detect patterns and find their own preferences within musical styles. If they never hear it, they might not ever fall in love with it.

If your child shows a passion or promise with an instrument, they're more likely to stick with it through the initial learning curve if a parent (or grandparent or other relative) plays along with them. It's also a chance for the budding musician to learn outside of teaching sessions.

GIVE YOUR KID A HAIRCUT AT HOME

You can do a simple child's cut at home, quickly and free.

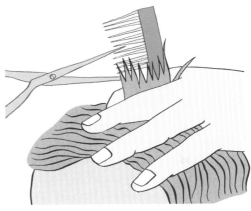

Start by cutting a head hole in a large garbage bag to create a barber's poncho. Gather hair-cutting scissors (preferably long and short versions), a spray bottle filled with room-temperature water, and a fine-tooth comb. Distract kiddo with a reader or tablet or something similar that will hold attention for the duration of the cut.

Sit him in a high seat where he is comfortable and you can work without uncomfortably bending over. Wet the hair with the spray bottle and comb it out. Start at the back of the head and have the "patient" look down and lean his head forward. Pull a section of hair down between the index and middle finger (the "barber's hold") on the hand without the scissors. Cut it to the length you prefer, then continue until all the hair is the same length along the neck.

Move on to the top of the head, combing the hair from top-back to front. Work your way to the bangs, using the barber's hold to pull up inch-wide sections of hair, and clip the ends all the same length. When you get to the bangs, have the child look straight ahead being very still and close his eyes. Now pull a section of hair down over the center of the forehead and cut to the desired length. Continue working outward in both directions so that the bangs are even across the width of the forehead.

Finish by cutting the sides, top to bottom and back to front, just as you did the top. Clean up around the ears as necessary (usually the hair directly over, behind, and in front of the ears will need to be cut shorter than the rest to look sharp).

Inspect your work and clean up any long strands or sections you missed. Carefully remove the poncho and clean up.

MAKE THANK-YOU NOTES FUN (AND A HABIT)

You're a gentleman. You know how gentleman (and gentle ladies) behave. It is part of the heritage you will pass on to your offspring, and it includes thank-you notes. This convention is becoming a lost art form, except among people with oodles of class— like you and your kid.

Make the exercise of writing and sending thank-you notes fun rather than drudgery for the little one. Start from an early age, with the rule that before one full day has passed, the bumble has to write a thank-you note for any present received. That's the only rule. The format is flexible: doing the entire thing in pictographs, adding cutout shapes, using weird paper, or indulging creativity in any other way. The thing has just got to include the words "thank you." Your child can even take a picture, print it out, and write on the back. Who knows? It may be so good that your child gets a "thank you" for the thank-you note!

MAKE KIDS DIRECTOR OF THEIR OWN MOVIES

Why not discover the little movie director in your house? It's easy to forget how fabulous the wondrous technology of our modern world is, but your kid doesn't need much more than a smartphone to start creating his own cinematic movie. It will probably be your phone, so you'll be the assistant director.

Start with your kiddo's idea. He needs to make a bare bones script that can be as simple as designating what his movie is going to be about. Then he can start shooting and collecting scenes as time and opportunity permit. Once he's collected a fair number of video files, help him download them to your computer and use either the native software or buy an inexpensive video-editing package (there are versions available just for child directors). Help him consider how movie shots are framed by watching films with him. Even shorts will give him some idea of composition, transitions, and editing.

From there, all he has to do is cut and paste to create his own little masterpiece. Then it's just a matter of setting up the red carpet for the premiere.

PACK THE PERFECT SNOWBALL

In a snowball fight, the perfect weapon is key. Any dad worth his salt will gift his junior warrior the precious knowledge of the perfect, aerodynamic snowball. All it takes is a little attention to detail, pride in craftsmanship, and good snow.

Find slightly warm, wet snow. The snow has to be a little wet, because powdery new fall won't hold together well. Gather snow deep below the surface or close to buildings.

Be responsible. No dirty snow, no small rocks or chunks of ice. And no throwing snowballs at vehicles, windows, or people who ain't involved in the Great Snowball War.

Use your fingers. Mittens don't cut it. You need the dexterity of fingers. Form the initial shape by rotating a large handful of snow around and around as you firm it. Once it's solid and evenly round, use your fingers to apply increasing amounts of pressure toward the center, from all sides. The snow should squeak if you're doing it right. When it becomes difficult to compress the ball any further, you've got your weapon! Repeat until you have a fully stocked armory.

TEACH YOUR YOUNGSTER TO SWIM

The ability to swim well is all kinds of useful, not to mention amazingly fun. Teaching a future aquatic master to swim starts with a strong focus on safety. First lay down the rules of the water for your young one, including no going in a pool without adult supervision and the mandatory use of a personal flotation device until the child is a demonstrably proficient swimmer and comfortable in deep water. As for yourself, never be further than arm's length from your swimmer in training.

A pool noodle or similar floating toy and a kickboard are key to teaching young swimmers. Start the lessons by working on treading water. Have the child put his arms over the pool noodle, keeping his legs pointed downward and kicking to slowly rotate in circles. Once he has practiced this quite a bit, graduate to hold the child's arms with just enough support to keep him above water while he treads without the noodle. Start the actual swim instruction when you're satisfied that your child can tread water by himself for an extended period.

Have him use a kickboard to support his upper body and propel himself by kicking his feet. When he has gotten comfortable with this process, he can begin submerging momentarily. Have him extend his arms, put his face underwater, and kick his legs to propel himself. He should do this for increments of five seconds, pulling the board back under his chest to come out of the water. (Any child will have an easier time of submerging his face if he is wearing goggles.) It also helps to give the student a distraction activity, such as blowing bubbles while his face is submerged.

When he can do all of that fluidly, float alongside him, holding him without the kickboard, as he moves his arms in tandem with his feet in actual swim strokes. This will take a good deal of energy, and you should hold your kiddo after a few feet, to allow him ample time to rest. Finally, when he's proficient at keeping himself afloat, he can attempt to coordinate his swim stroke with raising his face to the side to take a breath of air as he moves forward.

SHOW YOUR KID HOW TO THROW THE PERFECT SPIRAL

It's a rite of passage for every young athlete, a hallmark of achievement: the perfect spiral. A well-thrown football, spinning on axis, is a thing of beauty. It's also easier to catch and more accurate than a pass that wobbles. Teaching your kiddo how to throw one is an essential part of giving him an edge on the playground.

Start with the grip. The correct grip for a spiral is with the pinkie and ring finger on the laces, between cross stitches. The index and middle finger should be close to the end of the ball (which will be the back as it's thrown).

Stand right. The passer's shoulders should form a line pointed at the target. The front foot should also be pointed at the target, while the rear foot should be perpendicular to the front foot (the two forming a "T"). The knees should be slightly bent, and the legs should be kept springy, not stiff or locked out.

Set the throwing motion. The throwing arm should be cocked with the ball at ear level and the elbow at shoulder level or slightly above. The front hand should be held straight out, with the fingers pointing toward the target.

Throw. For the actual throw, the passer steps toward the target to begin a corkscrew release of energy up from the legs, using the hips to create torsion for the throw. The actual power in the throw is generated by forcefully torquing the whole body. The front elbow should come strongly back as if elbowing someone behind the passer, and the throwing arm should come forward through the throwing motion, with the eyes kept on the target.

Release and follow through. At the moment the ball is released, the weight is shifted onto the front foot, and the ball is spun off the fingers, with the back two fingers the last to let go. Just as the ball leaves the hand, the wrist is flicked and flung downward toward the opposite hip. The force in the wrist flick determines how tight the spiral will be and how fast the ball will spin.

CRAFT EASY, QUICK, CHEAP, AND FUN
HALLOWEEN COSTUMES

If you're going to do Halloween right, you have to make an original costume. Sure you could buy one for your bumble, but that's wasted money because next year, he'll want to be something else. The best costumes are ingenious and upcycle common household materials.

Start with the material. A large cardboard box can be the start of many different wonderful costumes. Paint it silver, cut arm and head holes, and glue on very various

wires, plastic pieces, and electronic leftovers and—voilà!—a robot! Or glue a grid of plastic cups mouth-down to one side, cut arm and head holes, and paint it all one solid primary color to turn your kiddo into a popular plastic brick.

A sheet can be a lifesaver last-minute costume: the ever-popular ghost. Just cut eyeholes. Or cut an old sheet into long strips, which can be glued together to create a classic mummy outfit. Let your imagination and the materials on hand guide you and don't be fussy. Remember that the costume has to last only one night—and one Halloween.

START A BOARD GAME NIGHT

The true Dadskills dad knows that traditions are key to wonderful family memories and bonding with the kiddos. The great thing about playing any board game as a family is that there is normally a little downtime between turns, which can be used for casual conversation. With her defenses down, a little one often opens up more than she realizes and may give you a ton of information about what's going on in her life. Board games are also an excellent alternative to screen time, one that incorporates more healthy human interaction. The key, of course, is choosing the right board game or games. (The little one should be included in that decision!)

Choose a day and time that suits everyone's schedule and that you can be fairly certain everyone will be able to make. Then look for games that will not only be entertaining but will also build skills.

Word games. Scrabble and Boggle are both good fun for thoughtful language development. Buy junior versions to ensure the kiddo has a fighting chance. You should also consider dialing back your competitive instincts, because if a kid feels radically overmatched in a game, she won't find it enjoyable.

Math games. Yahtzee is not only a fun, fast-paced game combining both luck and strategy, but it can also build basic math skills and help your little one get comfortable working with numbers.

Creative games. A game like Pictionary fires up the young imagination and refines simple art skills. There are several other family-friendly (and many that aren't) board games involving drawing or similar conceptual activities.

Physical skills games. Puzzle and building games such as Jenga and Suspend work on a child's fine dexterity and spatial and three-dimensional visualization skills. Plus they go fast in relation to other board games.

Classic strategy games. If it's just you and the kiddo, don't dismiss chess as a possibility. It combines advanced thinking, planning, and close observation. Even Battleship hones memory and strategic skill.

Keep in mind that any game goes better with snacks and drinks. Once your young game player gets used to store-bought games, consider the next step of helping her create her very own board game!

RAINY DAY HOPSCOTCH OR TWISTER

Dealing with more than one bumble on a vacation day or a play date can be a challenge, especially when bad weather confines everyone inside. The answer is simple—a few sheets of construction paper, some painter's or masking tape, and a few bottle caps or pennies! Use these to quickly create a challenging, engaging, and energy-burning classic children's game: hopscotch.

Number different colored sheets 1 through 10, then lay them out starting with square "1": three stacked; two side by side; one stacked; two side by side; and two stacked. Tape each square to the floor and to each other. Although it's best if the floor is solid, the tape should hold even on low-pile carpet.

A player drops his cap or coin into the first square, hoping over that square and following the pattern up and back without hopping out of the pattern or falling. He stops, balancing on one foot to pick up his cap or coin, and hops over the square. His turn continues as he tries to throw the coin or cap into the second square and repeats the process. His turn ends when he misses the square with the coin or cap or hops out of the pattern.

MAKE A HOMEMADE PUNCHING BAG FOR KIDS

Even kiddos need a way to work out a little anger or frustration. That's why a durable, kid-sized punching bag can be a great craft project. It can be assembled from recycled materials easily found around the house.

Use an old rug, retired yoga mat, or carpet remnant. It should be roughly 2' × 4' (61 × 121.9 cm). Roll up the rug loosely so that the pile is on the inside; duct tape it closed, leaving a significant cavity in the middle. Stuff a large garbage bag down into the cavity—bottom at one end and open mouth at the other. Pour or scoop sand or fine dirt into the garbage bag, until you've filled it up. Tie the top closed, fold up the extra, and stuff it in the end. Duct tape over the opposite end.

Buy a round pad eye with ring from the hardware store and push the pad down into the open end of the roll. Duct tape it in place securely. Finally cover the punching bag in a couple layers of duct tape. Hang it with chain from whatever support is convenient.

GO BACKYARD CAMPING

You need to show your offspring that adventurers like Bear Grylls ain't got nothing on you. More important, it's never too early to give kids an appreciation of the great outdoors. The place to start is camping. But before you test your child's rugged outdoorsy-ness, let him stick his toe in the water by camping in the backyard.

Backyard camping is a great way for young children to learn the pleasures and wonders of spending a night outside, without the homesickness and trepidation that can come from a first camping trip.

Start your trip off with a tent. The easiest option is a simple store-bought model made for quick setup. But don't shy away from making your own. You can create a legitimate teepee with half a dozen long, thin sturdy branches or even long tool handles and a plastic painting tarp or lightweight blankets (be forewarned that sleeping room will be at a premium). You can even drape a blanket over a low, sturdy tree branch and secure the sides with rocks to create a simple and quick tent.

Fire is a great addition to any backyard campout, as long as it's safe. Relocating a metal freestanding firepit is an easy solution, although you can build a credible-if-small fire in a large terra-cotta pot. However, if you do without the fire, it will be easier to stargaze and get your child get used to just enjoying the dark.

A meal, or even snacks, is a great idea, because it will give your little camper the full experience of what true camping will be like (no kitchen in the wild). Bring easy-to-make-and-eat finger food such as sandwiches, string cheese, and cookies rather than attempting a cookout.

Once bellies are full, bedrolls are laid out, and everyone is happy, teach your youngster to relax and simply enjoy the great outdoors. Look at the stars, tell stories, or play simple games like Telephone (if there are more than two of you) or Name That Tune by humming. The one hard-and-fast rule should be no electronics allowed.

WHIP UP SOME SLIME

Paging Science Dad to the lab! What better way to inspire a love of all things chemical than to re-create a classic formula: the recipe for slime. You don't have to be a scientist like Bill Nye to get this one right. It's easier than making chocolate chip cookies.

Slime is a perennial favorite among kids. As toys go, it's a little one-dimensional, but that doesn't seem to bother youngsters. Playing with a snot-like substance is predictably endlessly fascinating.

There are many ways to brew up a batch of slime, but the formula here is perhaps the easiest. Be aware that the more the slime is worked and played with, the tougher it will get. At a point, it will behoove you to brew up a new batch.

Start by pouring about 1 ounce (29.6 ml) of white glue (like Elmer's) into a metal bowl, and adding ½ cup (118.3 ml) of warm water. Add food coloring to achieve the desired color. Use a stir stick like those offered free at home centers to mix the two ingredients. After about 30 seconds, add in ¼ cup (102.3 g) of detergent booster (Borax). Depending on his age, you should let the kiddo do this and have him watch for the change in consistency and the reaction between the two ingredients.

Once the mixture becomes a little stiff, set aside the stir stick and use your hands (or the little one's) to knead the maturing slime. This can be a bit messy, so wearing latex gloves is not cheating and can save some cleanup. Once the slime is one uniform color and texture, it's ready! Discard any leftover water in the bowl. Caution children that they should never put slime in their mouths. Your slime lover can either begin playing with it, or you can put it in a large resealable refrigerator bag and refrigerate it for later.

The science lesson for the young student is fairly basic: The glue is what's known as a "liquid polymer." By adding water, you dilute it, essentially loosening the molecular structure. The added borax molecules physically attach to and link the polymer molecules into what can be considered one long polymer chain.

BUILD YOUR OWN WATER GUN

Using PVC pipe scraps and a few hardware store items, you can craft a water gun that will last virtually forever. Much of the fabrication has to be done by an adult, but an eight-year-old or above can assist.

Grab lengths of 2" and 1¼" PVC pipe, a 1¼" PVC coupling, 1¼" cap and tee, 2″ caps (three of them) and tee, and a 1 ¼" x 1.6mm″ O-ring. Find silicone grease and PVC primer and cement. Cut 8¼", 13", and 6" sections of the 2" pipe, and 22", 2", and 6" sections of the 1¼" pipe. Sand all the pipe edges perfectly smooth.

Measure and mark the center of a 2" cap. Drill out a centered hole with a 1¾" hole saw. Sand the edges of the hole perfectly smooth. Cement the 1¼" cap to one end of the 2" x 1¼" section. Work the O-ring over the open end of the pipe, so that it is snug against the lip of the cap.

Cement the coupling to one end of the 22" x 1¼" pipe. Cement the open end of the 2" section into the open end of the coupling. Cement the 8¼" x 2" section into one side of the 2" tee and the 13" x 2" into the other. Cement one end of the front handle into the open inlet of the tee. Drill a ¼" hole in the center of the second 2" cap (this will create one direct stream of water from gun; for a more diffuse spray, drill a triangle of ⅛" holes, or any combination). Cement the cap onto that end of the barrel. Spread silicone grease around the inside of the open side of the 2" barrel. Slide the 1 ¼" plunger assembly, O-ring side first, into the opening in the 2" barrel. Push the plunger all the way into the barrel.

Very carefully cement the center-hole 2" cap onto the back of the barrel, sliding it over the plunger assembly without getting any cement on the plunger. Cement one side of the 1¼" tee onto the back of the plunger. Cement the 1¼" handle into the nipple of the tee. Cement caps onto the end of the 6" x 1¼" section and the end of the 6" x 2" section. Test the water cannon out by depressing the plunger as far as it will go, immersing the nozzle of the barrel into a bucket of water, and slowly drawing the water in by pulling the plunger back. Then blast away!

Note: Use 50 mm and 32 mm pipe for 2" and 1 ¼" pipe, respectively. Couplings, caps, and tees should be adjusted accordingly. When making cuts, multiply inches by 25.4 to convert to millimeters.

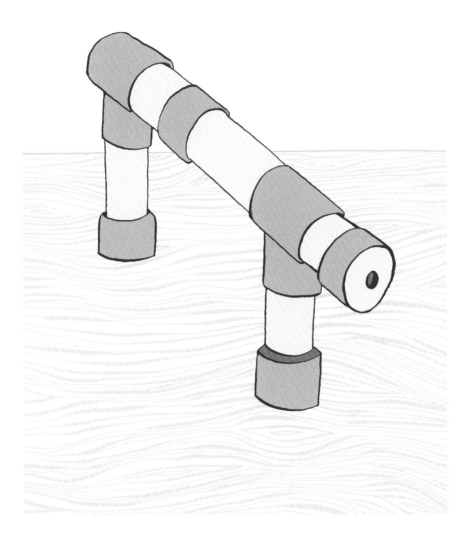

4

Roll with it,
Dad,
roll with it.

CHAPTER 4

Managing the Tweens

Yes, you may be capable of rewiring a room addition, learning a foreign language, or mastering calculus, but trust this: The wonderful child development stage known as "tweens" is going to leave you a little befuddled. Roll with it, Dad, roll with it.

The tween stage is generally defined as that period in a kid's life between ages eight and twelve. The stage is named rather obviously because it is right between pure childhood and teenager-dom. It's neither and it's both, which is what makes it such a challenging time for youngsters and parents alike.

The theme word for this stage is *change*. A kid's body is changing, there's usually the transition to a new school in the offing, relationships with peers and siblings is evolving as the youngster attempts to figure out his or her identity through the group he or she associates with, and the child's relationship to his or her parents is changing as he or she tries to balance the need for reassurance and support with the desire for more independence.

Phew. And you thought the toddler stage was a challenge for you!

The key here, as with so many other stages in your child's life, is patience. Your kid will be chafing against rules because of a desire for more freedom and a struggle with increasing responsibilities like more demanding homework. Add wild hormone fluctuations into the mix and the best present you can give your tween is allowing them to be a little difficult without always being punished for it.

That said, this is the ideal stage to set in place positive behaviors and essential life skills that will serve your kiddo for life. Teaching simple practices like balancing a checkbook or how to act properly during a job interview seem like small things, but they are the type of life skill that can fall through the cracks if parents don't take the care and effort to teach them.

Of course, this is also a chance to have a different type of relationship with your youngster and reinforce the notion of home as fun and enjoyable, a sanctuary of sorts. As an above-average dad, you want to make sure you maintain the bond with your youngster, and that's best done with shared fun activities. They can be as simple as a pizza night or something more involved like a trip to the beach to surf together.

MAKE A CHALKBOARD WALL

In terms of combining pure fun with usefulness, you'll be hard pressed to top a chalkboard wall. It's a cool look and a high-profile surface on which to leave reminders. It can be a handy pad to work out homework problems and just an enjoyable creative outlet.

You'll need chalkboard paint (available at any home center, paint center, or large hardware store). Wall prep is just as important. Depending on the child and the room, you may want to limit the chalkboard surface to a square or rectangle on a larger wall. Your kiddo needs to be able to reach it. Repair wall cracks, holes, or imperfections. Chalkboard paint looks best on a perfectly smooth surface. Mask off the area with painter's tape, prime it with a quality flat primer, then paint two coats of chalkboard paint on top.

Your little one can write on the wall as soon as the paint is completely cured (check the manufacturer's recommendations). Hang a piece of chalk tied to a string or put up a shelf or wall pocket to ensure that there is always chalk handy.

SET UP A USEFUL CALENDAR

Remember when wall calendars were a regular thing? Yeah, most people don't. But for some people, they still are, and they are just as useful as they always were. In this digital age it's easy to downplay the value of paper and pen, but an oversized wall calendar can save your kid's bacon and help her get super-organized (making your life easier in the process).

The trick is to mount this calendar where you child will see it every day. It needs to be hung at eye level, whatever that is for your kiddo: a wall over the bed in your child's room or even over the kitchen table if the tween sits at the same place and stares at the same wall every day.

Use a desk-blotter calendar; these are large enough that the space allotted for each day provides plenty of room to note essential events. Most also have holes at the top, making the calendar perfect for hanging. The more colorful the calendar is, the better. The goal here is to draw the eye again and again.

Attach one end of a string to the calendar with a thumbtack or glue and tie the other end to a felt-tip pen (the string needs to be long enough that the pen will reach all parts of the calendar and won't interfere with tearing of a monthly page). You and, hopefully, your child can use the pen to mark important events on given days. Attach different color pens to mark different types of events (school tests and important deadlines in one color, social events or family obligations in another).

From there, it's just a matter of getting your not-so-little one into the habit of not only checking the calendar each day but also adding her own listings. Important dates such as exams and term paper due dates are a given. But if your kid has chores she needs to do, listing them on the calendar is one more step in ensuring she doesn't forget them. Even if she fights back against the idea of the calendar, stick with it; eventually, she'll come to use it and appreciate it.

SET AN ALLOWANCE

You may have grown up earning allowance for specified—or unspecified—chores or responsibilities. Seemed like a logical idea, right? Tie work to pay. Current thinking about allowance, kids, and money is different. Make allowance a teaching tool and a positive experience for both kiddo and parent by following basic, logical guidelines.

Don't make it a transaction. Sure, you'd love your child to be more disciplined about the responsibilities you give him. But most experts believe that a quid pro quo exchange of allowance for chores isn't necessarily a healthy thing. Child development pros contend it sends the wrong message and that kids should tackle chores because they are part of the child's role in the family. The allowance will be your acknowledgment that you want your child to enjoy life and be able to buy the modest treat for himself once in a while.

Spend smart. Allowance is an excellent teachable moment. Before the first allowance is paid, communicate any rules for what he can and can't buy with it, and perhaps even a requirement for saving a small part of the allowance. A good way to make saving painless is to help him plan for a larger purchase, like an expensive video game. Have your kiddo budget and work out how long it will take to purchase the game given different rates of saving.

Make it reasonable. Setting the allowance amount can be tricky. Your kid's friends may get a certain amount, but outside influences should not determine a decision that is wholly yours to make. A common rule of thumb is one dollar for every year of age, but that does not necessarily apply to you or your household. You need to accommodate your own budget. Pay an allowance that is reasonable not only in a given week but considering the total over a year.

Offer bonus opportunities. Reinforce a work ethic and lessons in the value of money by offering payment for special projects that aren't covered under the child's regular responsibilities.

DESIGN A CLOSET WITH THE KIDDO

Does your kid's room look like it was hit by a clothesnado? Take heart; you are not alone. Most parents fight a never-ending battle against kid's room messiness, but you can institute a big step in helping your little one stay neat and tidy and make his room look more unique. Enlist him in setting up and organizing his own closet and you imprint the idea that everything has its place and should be put there when not in use.

Take the doors off. Silly as it might sound, you want to remove any potential impediment to your child properly storing clothes and accessories. Where kids are concerned, out of sight often means out of mind. They will often drop something on the floor rather than go to the trouble of opening a closet door and storing it. Enlist your child to help you remove them as the first step in getting him involved.

Make it cool. A closet isn't a sports-figure wall mural, but it can still appeal to the youngster's aesthetic. Paint the inside of the closet in vibrant colors or your child's favorite hues. Don't be afraid to let him go a bit wild with this part of the project—it's the inside of a closet for goodness sake! Take the kiddo with you when you go shopping for storage containers and let him make the choice (as long as the size is right). The more decisions the child makes, the more he'll own the closet space.

Mix up storage types. The most common mistake parents make with a child's closet is too much hanging space and too little of other types of storage. Typically most of the clothing kids wear can be folded. That means shelves, baskets, and hooks often serve the purpose better than hanging rods.

Label, label, label. The advantage of having a school-age kid who can read is that you can blatantly label where things are supposed to go. It's not a guarantee that cleats will make it onto the shoe shelf, but it's a start. Cool fonts and funky stenciling can also make labels a personalized graphic element.

GO DIGITAL WITH PLANNERS AND CALENDARS

It's trite, but it's true: The big curse of modern parenthood is the advent of the "screen." If your youngster isn't looking at a TV, computer, or tablet, she's likely checking out a phone (unless you've nipped that one in the bud). You fought the battle to have your kid look at you when you're engaging in a conversation, but now here is a chance to flip the script and make the digital environment work to your parenting advantage.

Just about any smartphone or computer has a native calendar—and most are transportable, working across devices. Online services offer other versions. Point is, those assets are there for the exploiting, and what better way to use them than to keep the kiddo on schedule and in the right place at any given moment. By scheduling events electronically or watching as your child plugs them in, you can set alerts and notifications. It works for tasks small and large; from studying for a math test, to taking out the garbage, to picking up a gift for her mom's birthday. It's hard for a child to accidentally miss a loud, annoying digital reminder (or multiple alerts), and those electronic pokes in the ribs take some of the burden off you.

TEACH YOUR KID COLOR CODING

Your dad used to say, "Don't reinvent the wheel." Good advice and counsel you can pass on in the form of a color-coding organization system. Color coding for organization has been around for as long as there have been colors. As basic as the premise is, most kids wouldn't think of it themselves. So introduce them to the concept to help them get their lives in order, for now and the future.

The idea is easy to grasp: Colors provide a hierarchy, and any system needs a key. They can color-code with vibrant binder inserts, with folders in different colors, or by marking things with colored markers. Color coding can be used as a system for homework assignments, household chores, special occasions, and more. Just make sure your kiddo makes a key so she knows what each color denotes.

DECLUTTER WITH A KID'S YARD SALE

Rug rats? More like pack rats. Chances are your kiddo's room is chock-full of toys, extra clothes, and more. And then there's all that baby and toddler stuff in boxes in the attic or garage. Time for a good cleanout! A yard sale is a quick way to do that. Enlisting your tween is the chance to teach him valuable life lessons about interpersonal transactions and money.

Plan. Help your tween discriminate between belongings to get rid of and those he wants to hold on to. Have him pull out boxes from storage with sellables. He can also invite friends to have their own tables—more vendors equals more customers. Decide on opening and closing hours.

Advertise. The more the better. Have your tween make signs and put up a listing on a classified ad website such as Craigslist.

Set up. Work with the young sales executive to set up displays and decide on pricing (the lower the better). It's easier to mark a whole shelf of items rather than individual pieces.

Mind the "store." Hard-and-fast rule: Once the sale starts, your tween doesn't have the option of just taking off if he gets bored. He has to see it through.

Wrap it up. There will inevitably be leftover goods. Suggest donating them.

SET UP A TWEEN WORK SPACE

Maybe you don't think your tween needs a home office. Think again. A basic, well-outfitted and comfortable work space communicates how serious you are about your tween's schoolwork; he's also likelier to be productive in a dedicated work area.

Desk. Big is best? Not necessarily. Kids tend to clutter whatever space is allotted. A kid's desk needs just enough top space for his computer, and enough room to comfortably open a spiral-bound tablet and write.

Lighting. Bedroom lighting is usually an afterthought and often more decorative than useful. Add a dedicated and strong work light to avoid eye strain and make homework as easy as possible.

Comfortable chair. Ideally your tween will be spending hours at his desk working his way into a great college. An uncomfortable chair short-circuits the effort. An ergonomic office chair is a must.

Printer/scanner. You may already have a home printer, but having a dedicated unit just for your youngster makes it more likely reports will be printed out in a timely fashion.

Storage. It can be drawers in the desk, but your tween needs to have private space where he can keep paper, extra school supplies, and basic office supplies.

PREPARE TWEENS FOR FORMAL EVENTS

You may not be James Bond, but you know how and when to wear a tux. That kind of knowledge is key to getting by in polite society. It might not come into play often, but when it's needed, it's essential. Do your tween a solid and pass down your sophistication.

Dress appropriately. Kids—especially tweens—are allowed a bit of latitude regarding the rules of formal dress. Yes, a formal evening wedding means the tween boy must wear a suit with dress shoes and the tween girl must wear a dressy dress. But school dances, special family events, and even formal dinners allow for a more relaxed dress code. At school events, allow your tween to choose his own attire unless he asks for help. For everything else, a blazer and nice pants with a button-down shirt should be as much as you expect. Allow for fairly new sneakers in place of dress shoes.

Know when to gift. In most cases, your tween won't be required to buy, bring, or present a gift; that's still mom and dad's responsibility. But make them aware of what the gift is, what the thought behind choosing it was, and how important it is. That will prepare the tween for late-teen years and beyond. Teach the youngster to bring a present to any birthday or commemoration of a special event.

Dine with class. Many formal events are going to involve a sit-down meal, and that's a chance for your young bon vivant to show off understated class and refinement. Gentlemen rise when any woman leaves or arrives at the table. The man of breeding also pulls out a woman's chair when she sits down if a waiter or captain is not already handling that duty. If your tween is confused about what silverware to use, advise him to watch others at the table—and use silverware at all times rather than his fingers. A napkin goes on his lap when seated and on the chair when he gets up from the table. Silverware goes on his plate during the meal—crossed if he's still eating, side by side if he's done.

TRAIN YOUR TWEEN IN ANGER MANAGEMENT

You aren't a road-rage type of guy, so you're already a good example. But emotions often get the best someone who's staring down the barrel of puberty. Give your tween practical tools to help him manage troublesome angry outbursts.

Identify anger. Start by discussing anger with your tween. Can he show you a handful of anger? If not, it's not tangible—we create it, and we can stop it. Have him think about a time when he was angry and look at how that anger made him feel and how it seems now. Decoding anger is the first step to dealing with it when it happens.

Use the ten-second rule. Teach your tween to actually count to ten when he gets angry, before he takes any action or says anything.

Sanction self time-outs. Give your teen permission to remove himself from a situation or outburst, taking time to cool down in his room or another isolated area.

Provide a problem model. Anger is most often caused by a problem. Teach your tween to identify the problem and focus on solutions rather than simply indulging in briefly satisfying anger.

PREP YOUR YOUNGSTER FOR CAMP

The preteen years are probably the last time your kid will go to camp, so help her make the most of it.

Pack smart. Follow the camp's packing list and work with your tween to remember anything particular to her needs—medication, extra glasses, and anything that might head off embarrassment.

Mark possessions. Labeling everything your kid takes with her is crucial if you ever want to see it again. It's not that her favorite T-shirt will be nicked; things just get lost in the chaos of a bunch of tweens sharing a cabin.

Make sure the paperwork is done. Don't cause your kid or yourself stress by messing up the check-in because details fell through the cracks.

Be upbeat. Even the most secure kid is going to experience some trepidation and potential homesickness. Stay positive and point out all the fun and interesting activities she'll be doing.

INSTILL MANNERS

You're a worldly guy, and you understand that manners are the social lubricant that makes interacting anywhere a whole lot easier and more pleasant. You can never start too early, or reinforce too often, lessons in good manners. Even if it takes him well into his adulthood, your tween will eventually thank you.

Direct the behavior. Obviously it's great to model proper manners in polite society, but you can't always be sure that seeing translates to doing. That's why it's better to tell your tween outright how to behave. Rather than open the door for someone, discreetly suggest your youngster do it.

Reinforce good manners. Being polite will eventually become second nature to your child. Until it does, a little positive reinforcement goes a long way. Commend your tween's good manners when they are on display.

Start at home. It's very easy for tweens to fall into the trap of thinking manners are only meant for strangers. Insist that your child show good manners with older family members and neighbors.

Address the less obvious manners. Don't assume your tween will know what constitutes good manners in any situation. While it's one-and-done as far as teaching blatant practices like opening the door for someone, more subtle signs of mannerly behavior need to be addressed up front. Start with *no gossiping or talking dirt* about someone—in person or online. *Being punctual* is also something that defines good manners and a practice that seems extremely difficult for tweens to master—but you can definitely hit that point hard. Manners also extends to sports; it can be difficult for anyone wrestling with a hormonal transition to control strong competitive drive, but it's important that your child learn how to be both a good loser and a good winner. Lastly making fun of someone or bullying them in any way is the exact opposite of manners and should be the opposite of how you want your child to behave at school or anywhere else. Work with your kiddo on ways to avoid getting swept up in the peer pressure to do or say negative things.

LIVE TRAINING IN RESTAURANT ETIQUETTE

Celebrate, oh gourmet dad! Your offspring is at an age where he can reasonably accompany you to a decent sit-down, tablecloth restaurant. But first, you have to make sure he knows what he's supposed to do there. The best way to do that is to have a rehearsal: a sit-down, tablecloth restaurant experience at home.

The basics. Emphasize that women sit first. If the host doesn't do it, he should pull his mom's chair out for her. When seated, his napkin goes in his lap, not his collar.

Ordering. Drinks first! A tween can order a cola or a club soda, but mock drinks like a Shirley Temple are usually for younger children. Make sure he knows that it's okay to ask questions when ordering but that he has to wait until the server asks for his order. Teach him to hand his menu to the server after ordering.

Eating. All the regular rules apply: no elbows on the table, no open-mouthed chewing, and no eating with hands. Sit up straight and join the conversation. If he has to go to the bathroom, require him to say, "Excuse me," and put his napkin on his chair.

HONE DEBATING SKILLS

Yes, you can hold your own in a street fight if push comes to punch, but you're no slouch in a polemics brawl either. It's a skill every tween should pick for good reasons—both at home and on a debating club. Debate club looks great on a college application. Formal debaters start with an assertion, build reasoning behind that, and collect evidence to support their reasoning. It's a scientific process that offers many benefits.

Balance. Debaters become skilled in looking closely at both sides of an argument. Consequently their approach to any controversial issue is extremely thoughtful, understanding, and logical. That's not only good for the schoolyard argument about who is the better point guard or whether we should have a DH in baseball, but it's a skill that will serve your youngster well as he ages and goes forward in the world. We all encounter and need to resolve conflicts.

Analytical skill. Anyone who practices debate becomes skilled at analyzing data and breaking them down to form an argument. Analytical skills serve a tween through high school and beyond, often as an essential tool for acing college courses.

Listening. One of the most important and useful tools debaters use is their ears. If you're going to form a cogent counterargument, you have to listen closely to the finer points of the argument in the first place. Listening is a lost art form and a vanishing skill—one that will serve your youngster well in everything from romance to a job search.

Logic. Every argument in a debate has to proceed from one logical point to the next or it won't hold much water. The process of logical progression is a key component in writing a successful school paper or doing well on a written exam. It's also a good general skill to have if you don't want to make foolish mistakes in life.

Life skills. Debating skills generally translate well to everyday situations. Because the debater has to seek out evidence and be intellectually curious, he can be a great conversationalist. He also becomes a much better and more confident public speaker.

FOSTER INDEPENDENCE IN THE TWEEN

Ready to tread a fine line? Welcome to tweens and independence. Although they are not as reliant on you as younger children might be, the average tween is also not as capable as an older teenager of making judgment calls. So helping your kiddo become more independent is a matter of degrees and careful consideration on your part.

A big difference from younger ages is that the tween is most likely ready to stay home by herself. Most experts recommend starting this practice at age ten, but you have to make that decision based on your own comfort level and your child's maturity. Leaving a child home by herself opens up possibilities for you and your significant other. Who doesn't want a date night? But you have to set your tween up for success. Program emergency numbers into your child's phone and clearly name them ("the Joneses, emergency"). If your tween doesn't yet have her own phone— uh, independence? You also want to provide the home-alone creature with a clear list of "can dos" and "absolutely nots." Then it's the big leap of trust involved in closing the door behind you on your way out and fighting the urge to call every 10 minutes.

Trust is key when it comes to the drama in your child's life as well. Don't get involved in petty squabbles and disputes with friends and don't pry. You'll want to, because every parent wants to. Be careful about butting in with advice that wasn't solicited. A little restraint is a great way to create effective two-way communication going forward. Make it clear that you're always willing to listen.

Money is another key area where independence can be established. Tell your tween what your saving strategy is for her college fund and why you have one. Explain how retirement accounts work and the pluses and minuses of a savings account. If she wants to start one, you'll probably have to help her out but let her manage it from there. The same with cash on hand: Fight the urge to budget for your tween. She may make some bonehead purchases, but it's a small price to pay for learning experiences.

TEACH LAUNDRY BASICS

Laundry day will always be made easier if your tween is doing his own. A little succinct instruction will set him up with an essential life skill. Start by *telling* him that you're going to teach him how to do laundry. Don't ask, "Hey, you want to learn how to do laundry?" The answer will always be "No, thanks."

Labels. Show him where labels are on clothes and tell him to check them for special instructions and to determine fabric type.

Prep. Have him separate colors. If you have confidence in him, discuss further separating by fabric weight (towels separate from thin, lightweight shirts).

Machine cycles. Explain different cycles and the clothes that match them. Explain any special settings. If you use detergent "pacs," amount is easy. If you use liquid detergent, be specific on how to measure for each load. Kids generally overestimate the amount of soap they'll need.

Dryer basics. Explain the dryer settings and how to prevent shrinkage or other clothing damage. Dryer sheets or other instructions are probably TMI.

Special requests. Have him consult you or his mom with anything unusual, like a stain—and impress on him the fact that stains set once they go through the dryer.

HELP A TWEEN DESIGN A BEDROOM

Admit it—you loved coming home to a tidy, handsome home, one that reflects your style and taste. Showing that sense of style with design elements that make each room more welcoming and comfortable is how a house becomes a home. Give your tween that gift by letting him choose his bedroom style. It's where he can harmlessly express himself and experiment with who he is or who he wants to be. It won't cost much, and you can always redo the room when he flees the nest.

Of course, there are limits. For instance, you obviously can't allow structural changes, and for a number of reasons a ban on TV or other entertainment paraphernalia in the bedroom might be a good idea. (Unless you're cool with your kid cutting out the family and spending all his time in his tween cave.)

Paint. Paint is an inexpensive, easy, and profound way to personalize a room. Let your tween guide the whole process: picking a color scheme, looking at room schemes online or in magazines, picking up paint chips, and prepping and painting the walls. And, no matter what the final color scheme, remember that it's not for you. You can always leave the door closed.

Textiles. Bed linens and curtains can be pricey, so you'll need to set a price limit (or the option of using unusual choices—such as a canvas painter's drop cloth for drapes). If your tween happens to be handy with a needle and thread or sewing machine, he can customize plain versions that can be had for less.

Wall art. Well, maybe calling it art is a stretch. But let your tween go wild in picking and hanging whatever floats his boat: pictures he's shot, posters, prints from a yard sale—whatever.

Accents. The goal with accents is to add inexpensive, simple, and durable accessories to the room design. Let him choose some room jewelry, like lampshades, throw pillows, or rugs. If you or your partner is handy, or your tween is especially crafty, secondhand elements can be repurposed for room accents. It can be an ideal way to exercise creativity. It can also be a day of fun hunting for accessories and essentials at flea markets, online classifieds, and thrift stores. That can be a way for your youngster to find the funky or fabulous object that appeals to him without breaking the bank.

MAKE A CHORE WHEEL

No one likes chores, but the burden of chores is made lighter when shared. That's the secret behind the wonder of the chore wheel. Coincidentally the wheel itself introduces the concept of fun into tasks that are generally considered anything but.

Making a chore wheel is simple. Include your tween in the process to up the chance he willingly tackles the chores he draws. Use card stock, colored construction paper, or any thick paper. Draw three circles, each larger than the last by a significant amount (i.e., 4" [10.2 cm], 6" [15.2 cm], and 8" [20.3 cm] in diameter). Use bowls or a pencil compass to trace the circles and cut them out.

Divide the smallest circle into sections totaling the number of family members. Write a name in each section. Divide the other two wheels in the same number of sections. Subdivide those sections and write in time-consuming or big chores on the second smallest wheel, and smaller, less consequential chores on the largest wheel. Stack the three and use a tack to post the wheel on a bulletin board or wall. On a given day each week, spin the wheel to decide who will do what for that week.

TEACH PET CARE

Ooofa, you know the story: Youngster wants pet. Youngster gets pet. Parents take care of pet. It doesn't have to be that way; owning a pet can be an excellent way for a tween to learn essential lessons about responsibility.

Everyone needs to be honest about what they're getting into. A dog, cat, or parrot will probably still be alive when your child leaves for college. That means mom and dad are going to adopt the pet. (That's why a fish or turtle can be a good low-maintenance first pet for tweens.) Stay away from exotic pets because they are more hassle than they're worth and wild animals should be left in the wild.

The key to responsibility is culpability. The rule for a small pet like a fish is if it dies prematurely from improper feeding or care, no more pets. For a larger, longer-life span animal, a formal, written agreement is more effective. It should clearly state the tween's responsibilities and describe repercussions for violating them. This is a life we're talking about here! You child should take it as seriously as you do.

PREPARE TWEENS FOR EMERGENCIES

The chance that your child will encounter an emergency at some point is just a fact of life. Some dangers are natural, others man-made. But your child can be prepared for all of them with your help.

Natural disasters. Your geographic region may experience earthquakes, floods, tornadoes, lightning storms, or a combination. Prepare an emergency kit for your home, with your tween. In a large duffel bag, store first aid supplies, clean water (1 gallon (4L) for each person in the house), food (three days' worth of nonperishable items), a flashlight; battery-powered transistor radio, loud whistle, pliers, dust masks, and backup cell phone charger and batteries. Drill on what to do in case of a fire (stay low, move fast, get out of the structure, gather with the rest of the family in a predetermined place outside). Cover what to do in a bigger disaster, agree on a meeting place, know where and how to seek shelter during a specific disaster (go to the FEMA website for specific disaster information: www.ready.gov/kids), and discuss the plan if communications are down.

Active shooter. The modern reality is that parents have to prepare children for a worst-case scenario—gun violence at school. First emphasize how unlikely this is. Then advise *run*. Don't worry about belongings or calling police; sprint the opposite direction from noise, gunfire, and panic. Run as far as possible. *Hide*. If running isn't possible, your child should hide, preferably behind a locked door. Barricade the door and stay as quiet as possible—silence a cell phone. Good hiding places include classrooms with doors that lock, closets, and large lockers. *Fight*. The last recourse if trapped is to fight back by throwing and striking the shooter with anything within reach, the heavier the better.

Health emergency. Tweens usually don't have the physical strength to perform CPR chest compressions or the Heimlich on an adult or teen. However, you can teach a simple triage method that can save a life just as surely. Where someone is bleeding profusely, the victim can bleed out before help arrives. Tell your child to press a reasonably clean compress (can be a shirt or other garment) with all his strength onto the wound. It's a way to stop bleeding and possibly save the victim's life.

TEACH YOUR TWEEN CURSIVE

Sure, you might think teaching a kid cursive is like teaching her to hunt dinosaurs. But actually, there are good reasons to keep the art of good penmanship alive. Writing in cursive can develop new neural pathways and improve fine motor skills. It allows the student to write more legibly when using longhand is the only option. It also develops spelling skills and gets the child familiar with reading cursive, a useful skill for any college-bound student who might research a famous person's papers.

Cursive is developed by basic rote muscle memory. Using a lined pad, have your tween start by copying out lowercase cursive letters of the alphabet, ten to twenty times for each. Once she becomes proficient at that, move on to uppercase letters. After those are mastered, it's time to start practicing entire sentences and then whole paragraphs. It won't take long, but you should push her to make each letter as neat and legible as possible.

TEACH HYGIENE TO TWEEN BOYS

Do your kiddo a favorite long before he gets deep into the throes of puberty and teach him the finer points of self-care. His later self will thank you.

Clean hair. Stringy, greasy hair is a good look on exactly no one. Longer dirty hair can have a negative impact on facial and neck skin. Urge your young charge to shampoo his hair at least every two days. Buy a mild, unscented shampoo and you'll help him preserve essential hair oils and scalp health that will head off dandruff problems.

Clean hands. Simple handwashing prior to eating and every time he uses the bathroom is a small measure to take to prevent common illnesses. Get him in the habit of clipping his nails once a week as well.

Clean pits. Before puberty, tweens may actually not need deodorant; but it's wise to get them in the habit of daily use before they really need it.

Clean (kind of) skin. Too much stringent washing is as bad as too little for tween skin (overly dry skin can cause the body to make more of the oil that contributes to acne). Your kiddo should bathe or shower once a day with a mild soap.

PREP A TWEEN FOR A JOB SEARCH

Sooner or later your youngster is going to want a little coin of the realm for himself. The rule should be, schoolwork and grades can't suffer or the job goes. Help him toward employment by prepping him for an essential life skill: acing a job interview.

Dress for success. He doesn't need a suit to interview for a job at the local drugstore, but a neat and clean appearance says that your tween has got his act together. Counsel him to wear trousers, not jeans, and a button-down shirt—and to take a shower before the interview.

Conduct a mock interview. Nerves will get the better of anyone who's unprepared. Sit down with your junior executive and run him through a practice interview so he has all the right answers to any question a future employer might ask.

Send an artful thank-you. It's a lost art, the interview follow-up. But there's no way not to be impressed by a young person who sends a "thanks for the opportunity" email or card after an interview.

INTRODUCE A TWEEN TO KARAOKE

You're a fun guy. Everyone says so. But once your tween becomes a tween, he's likely to doubt that proposition. After all, you're part of a duo who forms the voices of authority in his life. Never fear: You can inject fun back into that relationship with the power of song.

Karaoke can be a wonderful way for the family to indulge a group activity away from the TV. It can be a party at home, a great activity for special occasions like birthdays, and can even include your tween's closest friends. There are other benefits as well, including, believe it or not, practical rewards. Singing in front of a small crowd gets kids experience in pushing beyond embarrassment. It can make them better public speakers. In the same vein, it's an excellent way for Mom and Dad to show they're human too. For all its cheesiness, karaoke can also hone kids' legitimate musical talent. A small karaoke machine won't break the bank, and it's likely to see a great deal of use right through your kiddo's teen years.

TEACH YOUR KID TO PROTECT HIMSELF

In the rare instance, your tween might find him or herself trapped by bullies intent on proving themselves by throwing another a kid a beating. If escape isn't an option, and you're not fond of advising your kid to take a beating that might lead to serious injury, you'll need to show the little one how to defend himself and fight back just enough to get away. It's all a matter of stunning the attacker so that your offspring can make a dash for freedom and safety.

First up, teach some basic self-defense. Fists should be glued to the chin so the arms are ready to block any punch. This will prevent dental and head damage—the worse possibilities in a fight. Next up, show them how to counterpunch and open an escape route. A simple, solid, correctly thrown and basic punch can halt the action just long enough for a quick escape to adult help or a run home.

A proper punch requires the whole body and involves an economy of movement. All energy is directed straight to the target. It starts with a solid base. The tween's legs should be shoulder width apart, knees slightly bent and legs kept springy. The weight should be balanced. Fists should be held right at the chin in a ready boxer's pose.

Start the punch from the feet, pivoting the back foot up on the ball and flexing the legs. The hips torque toward the target. The shoulders mimic the torquing action, and the punching arm extends at the last minute as the weight shifts forward. The arm should not loop out but, instead, take the most direct path to the target. The opposite arm should be kept tight to the body with the fist at the jawline, ready to block a counterpunch. The puncher shouldn't drop his eyes; they should remain on the target through the completion of the punch. He should punch through the target.

Have your tween work against a heavy bag and practice hundreds of straight power punches. Eventually he can build two- and three-punch combinations, but a single power punch will do the job in most circumstances. Drill him to keep his hands up, because the opponent may flail out in desperation.

AMAZE TWEENS WITH A CARD TRICK

Every once in a while, it's good to let the kids know just how incredible you are. A couple of solid card tricks will surely fill the bill. Card tricks are endlessly fascinating and fun, not just for kids but for adults as well. Don't be surprised if, after learning this one, you find yourself doing it for grown-ups as well.

The trick is simple but perfectly deceptive. While you're alone, count out twenty-five cards. Stack them on the top of a deck and use your fingernail to mark between the stack and the deck. In front of your audience, fan the deck, being careful to maintain your place at the bottom of the twenty-five-card section. Let your mark pick a card and look at it without showing you. Now pull off the top section and have him put his card facedown on the top of the rest of the deck.

Cap the deck with the twenty-five-card section and begin flipping over cards from the top. Silently count out twenty-five cards. The twenty-sixth card is one your mark picked. Stop when you turn it over and make a show of saying it feels like that is her card. And it is!

For the second trick note the top card of a deck (let's say it's the 5 of clubs). With your audience in place, shuffle the cards, being careful to keep the top card on top. Place the deck on the table facedown. Ask an audience member to cut about a third of the deck. Flip the cut so that those cards are faceup. Ask another audience member to make a second cut, equal to the first. Holding the first and second cuts, flip them over and place them back down on the deck, so that the second cut is now faceup. Slide off each of the faceup cards and the first facedown card will be the original top card. Peel it off and hold it up to the audience, announcing what the card is without looking at it.

INSTITUTE MAKE-YOUR-OWN-PIZZA NIGHT

If you're looking to win that "Coolest Dad of the Year" award, this may be your ticket to the podium. Homemade pizza combines fun, creativity, family time, and an incredibly delicious indulgence all in a package your tween will really appreciate.

The process is easier than you might think. Start with the perfect dough. Pour 1 ⅓ cups (315.4 ml) of warm water into a large mixing bowl. Open two packets of yeast and sprinkle over the water. Let it sit undisturbed for about twenty minutes or until actively foamy. Then mix in 2 tablespoons (25 g) of granulated sugar, ¼ cup (59.1 ml) of olive oil, and 2 teaspoons (12.2 g) of salt. Whisk together until completely combined, then dump in 4 cups (499.7 g) of all-purpose flour. Mix until it forms a dough.

Oil another large glass mixing bowl with olive oil and transfer the dough to that bowl. Sprinkle a little olive oil over the top of the dough, cover with plastic wrap, and set it somewhere warm and out of direct sun so that the dough can rise. Let it rise for around an hour or until it has doubled in volume. Remove the ball to a floured surface and knead lightly, then chop into four sections and roll into balls. Now the fun begins.

Set out a selection of toppings in bowls. These can be any of the family favorites, such as sliced pepperoni, mushrooms, onions, or other toppings. But the selection should include shredded mozzarella and piquant cheeses like formaggio. Fill one bowl with pesto sauce and another with tomato sauce—homemade or from a jar.

On the floured surface, each person flattens out a ball of dough to a roughly round shape, using fingertips (although tossing is permitted). Then each person in turn gets to scoop whatever toppings he or she wants. Place the pizzas in the oven either on a pizza stone or on a cookie sheet that is placed on top of an upside-down cookie sheet. Preheat the oven. Set the dial to the highest temperature (ideally around 500°F [260°C]). Bake the pizzas for twelve to fifteen minutes, until the crusts are crispy and golden and the cheese is melted.

OWN A PAINTBALL MATCH

It all comes out on the field of battle. Will you be cannon fodder or a medal earner? More important, will you let some ten-year-old drop you like fourth-period French? Or will you seize the day, own the match, and install a new respect for the value of experience in your son and his friends? When it comes to winning at paintball, it all comes down to doing the little things right and showing those other warriors how the big dogs do it.

If you've joined your tween and his friends for a match, be aware that those little kids may be weaker; but they are also smaller, more nimble targets. Pick your shots carefully.

Take care of your tool. You're only as good as your weapon. Yours should be clean and dry, especially the hopper. That's why you never pick up and reuse a dropped pellet. That's just asking for a gun jam.

Be aware of your fuel. CO_2 gun? Check your gas before battle begins and don't mess with the knob once it's set.

Slow the action. One slow bull's-eye beats ten near misses. Don't sacrifice accuracy for fast repeat shots—that's a rookie move.

Watch your weapon position. Paintball guns need to be upright to operate correctly. It's something to keep in mind when shooting from an awkward hiding hole and the gun is partially sideways—pellets may not feed correctly.

Aim and track. Don't just aim and shoot. Track shots to see how they're flying. Paintballs lose velocity and trajectory rapidly over distance. They will trail downward due to their weight. Adjusting shots for that is key to success.

Conceal and live. Cover is your friend. Don't expose yourself just to get a shot off.

Keep a 360-degree awareness. Keep your head on a swivel. Target fixation is one of the biggest errors among paintball-match losers.

Shoot still targets. Wait for your target to stop moving. It's immensely harder to shoot a moving target.

Use your partner. If you've buddied up for the match, fight back to back at all times and stay aware of where your partner is in space when he's on the move.

WAGE THE MOTHER OF ALL
WATER BALLOON BATTLES

You may not have a swimming pool, but that doesn't mean you can't beat the heat with your kiddo, along with all the tweens in the neighborhood. A good old-fashioned water balloon fight is a time-tested way to cool off, and fun for everyone who participates. It's also an excellent way to burn off excess tween energy.

When assembling the troops, the more the merrier. Make sure you have plenty of balloons and don't cheap out—discount balloons tend to break in the thrower's hand, which can be a heartbreaking disappointment. Fill all the balloons first and stockpile them in plastic grocery bags or other plastic carriers. Don't overfill the balloons or they may break long before they ever find their way to a target.

When conducting a water-balloon campaign, there are some rules of engagement to follow. These will guarantee that the battle is fun for everyone concerned without becoming a nuisance to the rest of the neighborhood.

Keep it to warriors only. The first rule of water balloon battles is no civilian casualties. If someone isn't formally involved in the battle, they are not fair game and are to be given safe passage. The rule that goes along with that is no property damage. A fully filled water balloon can break a window or damage a potted plant. Keep the battle on the field of battle.

Assess your squad. If you have some underage, tiny neighborhood kids, they may be your front line resupply agents or ambushers. Everybody should be given a role.

Have no winners or losers. Actions are enough. Limit the trash talking to avoid bad feelings during what should be a purely fun activity.

Use a safe word. Sometimes water balloon bombers forget when enough is enough. Give everybody who's participating a safe word to yell if they are overwhelmed, soaked, or just want to take a time-out.

Choose small ammo. Smaller water balloons hurt less and are more accurate. They are also easier and quicker to fill and still do a fair amount of soaking.

Finesse your weapons. Fight the temptation to overfill your balloons, because they may burst during the throwing motion.

SURF WITH YOUR TWEEN

Live within striking distance of an ocean beach? Then what are you waiting for? You can be out there shredding gnarly waves with the youngster, making forever memories and getting into top-notch shape.

It's hard to find an activity better than surfing for a whole-body workout that delivers tons of fun. It may even become a regular activity for both of you. Surfing is a great way to bond and spend quality time in the great outdoors. Follow these easy steps to help you both pop up the first time and ride like a pro.

Wait for yours. Tie on your ankle tie, make sure the kiddo's is secured as well, and paddle out to where the waves are breaking. Once there, you both need to sit on your boards rotating your feet in circles—the foot on each side going in different directions to keep the board pointed parallel to the waves.

Paddle into the wave. When the right wave comes, lie on the board and paddle for all you're worth. Paddle until you're sure you're in the wave; don't pop up early.

Push up. Set your hands next to your chest like you're doing a yoga "baby cobra" and get up on your toes as you would for a push-up.

Set the back foot. Slide what will be your back foot up equal to the opposite leg's knee and set it on the board, perpendicular to the length of the board.

Position the front foot. Step the second foot through your hands to right under your chest, putting it down at a slight angle to and cutting across the midline of the board. Your hands should still be flat on the board, and your torso should be perfectly straight with your gaze forward.

Pop up. Once your feet are set, release your hands and raise your chest and shoulders, facing the direction you're headed. Keep the body compact and the knees bent. Check your stance as you stand up a bit to maneuver the board. Your feet should be about 10 inches (25.4 cm) wider than shoulder width, with your weight evenly balanced between them.

5

Independence
is blooming,
and brother,
it is a rocky
process.

CHAPTER 5

Taming Teens

Surely you have only to think back to your own teen misadventures, sir, to understand what challenges await you in taming your own teenager. We all have a few regrettable incidents in our past, and many of those date to our teen years. It's to be expected during a life stage where a person inhabits the body and desires of an adult, with a mind that may not quite be there yet.

Good to always remind yourself that this is actually the final stage before true adulthood. No matter what, this is bound to be a busy time in your teen's life and, consequently, in yours. There is college to plan for (or alternatives), jobs to plan for, a future to plan for. There is a lot to look forward to but also a lot that must be done now for that future. That said, some of your most important work as a dad is in the here and now.

It's not like teens need no supervision. No, but unlike younger ages, the supervision has to be subtle, at a distance, and gently administered. Independence is blooming, and brother, it is a rocky process.

That's why a good part of this chapter is dedicated to dealing with the hard stuff, the big issues, head on. It doesn't make any sense to ignore them, because only trouble that way lies. You also need to help your teen build skills that he or she can use to pilot through this stage and through those to come. Those skills are essential, and they are where your sensitivity will need to kick into high gear. It's always an interesting practice trying to teach someone who is positive that you know far less than they do.

And during all of that? Well, you have to ensure both you and your child never lose sight of the fact that you are family—with a capital F. You haven't forgotten that this is the last stage before adulthood, which means (in most cases) the last stage before your fledgling flees the nest. You need to make sure you stay as close as ever, imbedded in your teen's heart as he or she is in yours. Frustrating, sure, but you never forget how much you love your bumble—even a petulant teen bumble.

HAVE THE TALK

No parent wants to have the talk. We don't like to think of our children as sexual beings. But a big part of the teen years is becoming exactly that. As soon as your kiddo heads into puberty, it's time to do the uncomfortable thing and sit down for the most awkward conversation you two are ever going to have.

It's not just about simple mechanics; today's complex media landscape leads to a lot of confusion about what sex is and isn't. Cut through the confusion and tailor your approach to your teen's gender.

WITH A BOY . . .

It's imperative at this formative stage that his role model—you—emphasizes women are human beings, equals, and people with needs, feelings, emotions, and all the complexity that men have. It's essential that he not objectify women.

Take on XXX. Whatever your position on pornography, it's healthiest for teens to stay away from it. Research has shown that porn can have a deeply negative effect on a teen's expectations about sex. Unfortunately your teen boy may be too embarrassed to admit that he's watched porn. Take any judgment and punishment out of the equation and make a clear case for why pornography is especially unhealthy.

Give the facts. As if the discussion isn't already uncomfortable enough, you'll need to question your son to determine if he has an understanding of basic sexual function and reproduction. It's crucial that you clear up any misunderstanding, and provide a safe and calm forum for your kid to ask potentially embarrassing questions.

Just say "No." The best starting point is to preach, "Wait till you fall in love." Explain that abstinence the most definite way to ensure against disease, unwanted pregnancy, and complicated relationship problems. But be realistic; statistically, most kids don't maintain abstinence, driven as they are by a flood of hormones. So you also need to be explicit about other safe-sex practices and birth-control.

WITH A GIRL . . .

A dad is often not the best person to have "the talk" with a daughter; a mother or female relative is going to better understand what the teen girl is facing and going through. That said, there may not be an option, or you may be part of the talk to back your wife up. Whatever the case, bring your sensitivity A-game, listen as much as you talk, and you'll get through it.

Be direct. Sweet mother of mercy, this is your daughter sitting in front of you. You'd like nothing more than to give her a hug, tell her you love her, and move on. But you have to man up and communicate directly and bluntly so that there is absolutely no misunderstanding.

Set the stage. Impress on her how much you trust her judgment and respect her as a human being. Explain that it is your responsibility to ensure that she is safe and happy, in that order. The point is to arm your daughter with whatever she might need to effectively and positively deal with any sexual situation. Tell her in no uncertain terms that she needs to be her own strong advocate for the type of attention she wants and doesn't want. A boyfriend, peers, society, or social media stars do not set the agenda for her body; she does.

Promote nonsex. As you would with a son, you should urge your teen daughter to embrace abstinence. That's no guarantee that she'll listen, but it's the best starting point. In any case, be adamant that she never consider having sex unless it's on her terms.

Take control, not just birth control. Your daughter has to understand that she is in control of any sexual encounter. If at any time in an interaction with the opposite sex she feels she is not in control, she needs to immediately get away from that individual. She also needs to be in control of birth control, even if that means directing her partner to use it. An unwanted pregnancy would impact her life more profoundly than it would her partner's.

Think safety first and always. Above all else, you must drive home the need for your daughter to never put herself or let herself be put into a dangerous or unstable position—around boys who have been drinking heavily, for instance. Sexuality is always a secondary concern to personal safety.

EXPLAIN BODY CHANGES

Oh, the wonders of biology. Young bodies change quickly once a child hits the teen years. The most radical change is puberty. Explaining to a teen what is happening can lessen the stress as the young mind fights to catch up with the maturing vessel in which it finds itself.

Teen boys will be surprised about the places hair is sprouting but most intrigued by the nascent facial hair. It's the perfect time to explain how to shave, including how to deal with sensitive skin. Because puberty is most marked by the ability to ejaculate, this is also the time to have the sex talk with your teen boy and demystify many of the topics that teens are often left to figure out for themselves. Reassure your kiddo that any vocal changes are transitional and will resolve within months if not weeks.

The teen girl will be wrestling with her own changes. As her body develops, she'll wrestle with newfound attention from boys. But the most dramatic change is the onset of a teen girl's period. The time to deal with that is not the first time she gets it but long before. And the person to brief her on it is not her dad but her mom or another female relative.

STOP YOUR TEEN FROM SMOKING OR VAPING

It doesn't take a Mensa membership to know all the truly devastating dangers of smoking. Problem is, tobacco companies (and vape makers) are experts at subtly marketing to youngsters. And yet, against all sense, teens still harbor an impression of smoking and vaping as cool.

That's a lot for a parent to push back against, but push back you must. There is so much riding on the success of your home-based smoking prevention campaign. It's not an overstatement that it could be a life-and-death issue.

Outlaw it. The first step is to draw a line in the sand before your teen ever finds himself at a party being offered his first smoke. Clearly state where you stand. Explicitly forbid your teen to smoke or vape. You don't have to spell anything out at the moment, but the implication is that there would be severe punishment for noncompliance. Be clear that you mean all tobacco or nicotine products—including those that can be chewed.

Maintain a good example. If you're going to successfully preach it, you've got to live it. If you or your significant other smoke or vape, quit. The facts are clear: Teens raised in households where at least one of the parents smokes are statistically much likelier to take up smoking.

Discuss the appeal. Be straightforward, honest, and open. Talk to your teen about why smoking and vaping might seem cool. Dive into what the attraction is in general and what your teen thinks about it. Then move on to the following point.

Explain the downsides. This could be a long, long discussion. The health risks associated with smoking are well chronicled. And it's not just a matter of the more serious issues like a higher risk of lung and other cancers or the potential for life-crippling COPD in later years. Also cover vanity issues, like how disgusting smoke-yellowed teeth and leathery skin are, how smoking dulls the hair and nails, and how the stink of stale smoke often permeates the clothing and belongings of smokers.

Hit the wallet. Add up what a year of a half-pack-a-day habit would cost. Lay that out for your potential puffer, and let her think about all the other things she could buy with that money instead. Also explain that smoking equals no allowance.

DEFUSE TEEN ATTITUDE

And you thought the terrible twos were bad. Come to find out, they can't hold a candle to the terrifying teens. Teen attitude is most often about control and testing boundaries to figure out what independence would be like. Unfortunately the immaturity of the stage means that there is no understanding about the responsibility that goes along with that independence. That's why you'll have to navigate a fine line between someone attempting to exercise his independence and a teen actually being disrespectful.

Avoid anger. As you did when your kid was a toddler, as much as possible take anger out of the equation. Sometimes, more than expressing himself, a teen just wants to see if he can elicit a reaction. If there isn't the response he wants, the bad behavior fizzles out.

Be judicious. Early on, decide what you'll allow and what you won't. Talk back? Witty replies? Swearing if it's not directed at anyone in particular? Establish your dos and don'ts and make them clear. But keep in mind that a bit of latitude gives your teen a chance to explore how he should handle different circumstances. It's his first step toward real adult independence.

Argue when necessary. You can't hope for an entirely conflict-free relationship. Occasionally he's going to catch you at the wrong time or vice versa, and it's going to lead to an argument. It's okay to air things out, as long nobody gets nasty or personal and he ultimately walks away knowing that you love and support him.

Introduce humor. Lighten up the situation whenever you can. This is a good way to prevent anything hurtful from being said and to defuse a tense situation. You have to be careful about timing it right, but humor can be your best attitude-fighting tool.

Be present. You can stop the elements that contribute to a bad teen attitude by being in close contact with your teen. The more you two do for recreation or just hanging out at home, the more the lines of communication are going to remain open. That will allow you both to address issues before they grow into problems.

HEAD OFF DRUG USE

Drugs are an unhealthy way teens handle life pressures and try new things. Heading off drug use starts with assessing if your teen is likely to use in the first place. Statistically teens are more susceptible if they already use alcohol or smoke, if there is history of drug or alcohol abuse in the family, and if they are struggling with schoolwork, bouts of depression, or poor self-esteem. Take steps to prevent your teen from ever starting drugs.

Close the gateway. Smoking and alcohol use can lead to drug use. Ensure your teen doesn't do either.

Monitor activity. Stay up to date on your teen's school and activities schedule, know where he is at all times, and—most important—know who he's hanging out with.

Tighten rules. If you suspect drug use, it's time to rein in your teen's independence and enforce curfews, rules about calling in, and other ground rules.

Play defense. Keep a close eye on your own prescription drugs.

Be a good example. If you smoke—or do drugs—in front of your teen, it's hard for him to take the no-drugs message seriously.

Be available. The more you interact with your teen, the more he'll know you're there to support him. He'll also understand that any drug use will quickly be detected.

IDENTIFY DEPRESSION OR MENTAL ILLNESS

All jokes aside, your teen's mental health is no laughing matter. Because it is already a tumultuous stage full of hormonal and other changes, along with the pressures of school and what comes next, it can be exceedingly hard to detect true mental illness versus just "normal" teen angst. The key is knowing what danger signs to look out for.

A vivid shift. Severe, sudden, or dramatic changes in your child's behavior and attitude can signal a problem. So can chronic sleep problems—either sleeping way too much (even for a teenager) or chronic insomnia from anxiety. Changes are especially worrisome if they are the polar opposite of how your child normally behaves.

Dullness. Teens tend to feel passionate about something—friends, hobbies, sports, or just annoying their parents. It is not normal for a teen to have no interest in anything and no apparent zest for life. If he cloistered himself in his bedroom, it's time to take action.

Body characteristics. Acute weight loss, a pale dull complexion, and most obviously any type of self-mutilation point to serious mental issues that need immediate attention. These can range from eating disorders to suicidal ideation.

Dire attitude. If your teen is openly and often expressing a lack of desire to live or the futility of his existence, making statements of hopelessness, or exhibiting signs of paranoia, he may be experiencing depression or another mental illness.

It's important to keep close tabs on your teen if he is experiencing serious changes to his mental outlook or physical characteristics. Some changes will be natural. You can best gauge by your interactions with your child. Even if they are unpleasant or unsatisfying, leave the communication pathways open and continue to press for communication.

If signs like these have you worried about the actual well-being of your teen, waste no time in getting him to your primary care doctor. The doctor will be able to give you a clinical assessment and refer you to the appropriate mental health caregiver. Be aware that if it comes to that, your teen may fight you on it. Push ahead. The mental illness can worsen rapidly and lead, in the worst cases, to suicide.

INSTITUTE ALTERNATIVES TO SCREEN TIME

It's the way of the world: Teens use electronic tools to socialize, communicate, interact, hang out, and do schoolwork. They are connected in ways that no generation before them has been connected, wired into the matrix. Maybe it's time to unplug them—at least a little bit.

If your teen's screen time or social media addiction has got you concerned, introduce alternatives. Require your high school student research at least one school paper in the library rather than online. You can further discuss ways to limit computer exposure in parent-teacher conferences with your student's teachers.

Regulations about screen time use can be a challenge to enforce, depending on which screen is the problem. Ban phones at the dinner table to start with and start a family board-game night once a week. Try keeping the home computer, tablet, and the like in rooms with minimal privacy—no retreating to the bedroom! If the problem is severe, consider replacing your teen's phone with one that doesn't provide internet access.

HELP YOUR TEEN SCORE GOOD GRADES

If you want a truly terrifying experience, check out the tuition of a top-tier college these days. Shoot, look at the cost of a not-top-tier school! It's rarefied air that you want your teen to ultimately breathe, and getting there starts with setting up a healthy college fund contribution—and him ponying up stellar grades. As if the college fund part of the equation were not enough, you should also play an active role in that grade thing.

Get involved. Attend every parent-teacher night, orientation, and parent information session, like those put together by the high school's college counselor. Come prepared with a list of questions and a pad and paper to take notes. Set up an appointment with teachers or a counselor if your radar picks up a problem. If you have the time and energy, you can consider volunteering at your teen's school, although this is a double-edged sword and may be counterproductive—embarrassing your teen for no good reason without giving you any additional information.

Access school resources. High school websites are becoming ever more interactive and information filled. Your teen's school may offer online listings of homework, assignments, upcoming college fairs, and other relevant information. You'll also want to avail your student of school resources such as special counseling for career tracks and tutors if she is struggling in any given subject.

Encourage nutrition and fitness. Learning works best when the student is healthy and alert. Start your teen's morning with something more than a cup of cafeteria coffee and a power bar. A larger nutritious breakfast sets the tone for the day. Ensuring that your teen's diet and health are top notch will be a good step toward high grades.

Create a workspace. An organized, quiet, well-lit workspace is essential for focusing on studies and homework. If your teen doesn't have that space in her bedroom, you need to establish it somewhere else in the house to give her the best chance of success on school assignments.

Communicate. The more you interact and talk with your student, the more likely you'll pick up on any problem with her studies before it actually impacts grades.

ADDRESS SCHOOL SHOOTINGS

You have to get your teen to that basketball game, track meet, or pool party. You have to make sure he's got his history assignment covered, has clean clothes for next week, and is healthy and happy. You have to check the college fund to ensure it's doing well and still juggle all the pieces of your own life. Doesn't seem fair that you have to make sure your kiddo isn't devastated or making himself sick with worry over the epidemic of school shootings, but there you go. The world can be a complicated and scary place.

The good news? The odds of your child being involved in an active-shooter situation are incredibly rare—below the chance of getting struck by lightning. But fear doesn't know reason, and it's wise to step in and make sure that's one worry that isn't nagging at your teen.

Take emergency precautions. First you need to take care of the practical. Be sure you know what your kid's high school's emergency procedures are and what role parents play in that. Also let your teen know the phone procedure to use when and if an emergency arises.

Be in tune. Pick up on signals that your teen is fixated on the dangers of school—if he is checking news stories about a school shooting several times a day, if he focuses on the event in any conversation, or if he seems overly worried about going to school. Look out for subtler signals as well, things that point to deeper disruptions in his psychology: sleeplessness, disinterest in food and other pleasurable activities, and a general unhappiness or similar severe personality change.

Facilitate communication within limits. It's imperative that you lend a caring ear to your teen's worries and concerns. Don't be afraid to discuss school shootings and your child's feelings around them but come back to the fact of how unlikely a shooting is to occur where you live or in your teen's school. However, at a point, bring the discussion to a close. Fixating on the topic can lead to even greater anxiety. For his own mental health, your teen is going to have to put the topic behind him and move forward.

PREVENT HIGH SCHOOL FIGHTS

You might have spent a few years learning the fine art of the squared ring, but as a parent you know that resolving conflicts physically is not okay. The only time physical action should be taken is to protect one's self or others from imminent physical harm. The often tougher but wiser course of action is to walk (or even run) away from heated conflict.

You teen may have a hard time doing that. If so, you'll have to take steps to curb physically violent behavior before the school does. A single physical altercation gone wrong could sabotage your child's entire academic future. Not to mention the liability if he actually hurt another student.

Careful communication is key. It can be jarring to find out that your child, this kid that you adore and have so much fun with at home, has been in a fight at school. The first order of business is to keep your cool. That will help your teen stay calm as he relates his side of the story. You getting mad or frustrated isn't going to help anything.

You also need to maintain an open mind and a clear perspective. Even if school authorities are punishing your teen, it doesn't mean they necessarily know the whole story. Give your teen a chance to tell his side completely and at his own pace. Don't make judgments as he explains it. Lead him forward by asking questions like, "And then what happened next?"

The key is to reinforce the point that any physical violence is wrong, without making your teen think the whole world is against him. Once you've ironed out what really happened and explained your position on violence in any case, it's time to take steps for going forward. Explain what could happen in a fight (someone could accidentally get seriously hurt, an academic career could be destroyed, charges and lawsuits could be filed). Then give your teen tools to deal with conflict situations. Tell him he needs to stay cool and walk away. If he is dealing with a bully or just a serial antagonist, he needs to bring the issue to a counselor or other school official.

DEAL WITH OBESITY

You may have been a high school superstar—captain of the football team, able to bench press twice your body weight and run a six-minute mile. Color everyone impressed. Your child is bound to be different from you, and you need to make it about him, especially if he's wrestling with unhealthy weight gain.

This is a matter of both physical and mental health. Obesity can become a lifelong condition and may contribute to totally preventable diseases such as Type 2 diabetes and chronic hypertension. But it can be equally devastating for the teen psychology. At a point in time when kids are searching for their own identity, it's extremely detrimental to wrestle with weight issues that often lead to bullying or less subtle, daily signs like social rejection.

You can help. Start with a visit to the family physician. The doctor will assess your teen's body mass index (BMI), a relative measure of fat to muscle. If your kiddo is actively growing, it may be a case of height catching up to weight. But if his BMI is high, take action. That involves changing the family lifestyle.

The goal should be losing no more than 2 to 3 pounds (0.9 to 1.4 kg) per week. Muscle should slowly replace fat, which may not result in a significant weight loss. Never shame a teen about weight. Focus on the positive and on health. Get him involved with regular activities. Long walks (thirty to sixty minutes at a brisk pace) are a powerful weight loss tool and help reduce mental stress. A game of pickup basketball or a long game of catch or tossing the football is productive.

The other side of the equation is food. This is where you can have a permanent impact. Ban sodas and high-fructose juices from the house. Water, sparkling water, or flavored waters should be the new habit. Eliminate snack foods and focus on healthy, filling meals that include diverse vegetables, abundant whole grains and complex carbohydrates, and smaller amounts of organic, low-fat proteins. Severely limit sweets and desserts.

Don't micromanage your teen or his weight problem; he has to do the work himself. Be supportive and surround him with healthy lifestyle options.

TEACH A TEEN TO DRIVE

Break out your kindest "father of the year" side, because it's time to give your teen the car keys and help him get mobile. Teaching a young person to drive is a rite of passage for teen and parent, and safety has to be the primary consideration at all times.

Driving instruction has five basic stages: *Vehicle awareness*—driver becomes familiar with basic operation and characteristics of the car; *fundamentals*—stopping and starting smoothly, parking, and simple spatial awareness so that he doesn't run into anything; *traffic navigation*—moving among other cars in motion and interacting with other drivers; *turns and parking*—U turns, three-point turns, parallel parking, and parking on a hill; and *challenges*—driving in inclement weather and at night.

Prep for success. Before he drives, have your teen exhibit knowledge and comfort with all the features he'll be using—turn signals, mirrors, and so on. Plan out a route of fairly deserted side streets and ensure he understands to respond to your commands at all times. Better he be embarrassed than get in an accident. Make sure the teen checks that the car is set up correctly—check mirrors, adjust belt and seat. Practice only during the day and in good weather.

Start easy. Find a large empty parking lot (or the deserted back section of a larger parking lot) and take your teen through the basics: smooth acceleration, smooth braking, turns, and spatial awareness.

Be chill. Don't bark commands and try not to let panic tinge your voice. Be clear and repeat a direction as needed but don't say it a hundred times. Give the driver lots of warning when you want him to turn or do something else. Regularly gently remind your teen to check mirrors and blind spots.

Play DMV tester. Sprinkle in questions while your teen drives (don't barrage him): "What's the speed limit for this section of road?" "Can you make a turn here on the red light?"

Practice harder techniques. Remember that the driving test isn't just driving. Work on parallel parking and Y turns as well.

Build on experience. Your teen needs to get used to traffic, so eventually move on to busy surface roads. Work on allowing ample space between cars and interacting properly with other drivers.

SHOW A TEEN HOW TO CHANGE A TIRE

Into every life a flat tire must occur. That includes your teen's. As you send him out into the big wide world driving a car to some far (or not so far) away place, make sure he knows how to handle the most basic of roadside breakdowns. Before he ever heads out, open the trunk and show him where everything is and illustrate how your particular jack is used to ensure safe operation. There's a good chance he'll never use the information, but if he has to, you want him to get it right.

Think safety first! The very first thing to teach your young driver is how to react to a flat tire. The car will become less responsive, and the situation should be fairly obvious. Tell him to pull to the side of the road as soon as it is safe to do so. Pull as far off the road as possible, onto a flat level area. Turn on the car's hazard lights and put out safety flares (you do have safety flares in the trunk, right Dad?) behind the car about 20 and 40 feet (6.1 and 12.2 m) back.

Prep the tools. Your teen needs to find the spare (usually an undersized "donut"), the jack (usually under the spare), and the tire iron (ditto).

Loosen and remove the flat. Apply the parking brake. Remove the hubcap, if any, and use the tire iron to "break" the lug nuts so that they can be removed by hand. Jack the car up (making sure that the jack is properly positioned under the frame of the car). Remove the lug nuts and remove the flat.

Put on the spare. Place the spare tire on to the lug bolts, and hand-tighten the lug nuts to secure it. Lower the car and use the tire iron to snug the lug nuts tight—in a star pattern if there are five bolts, and in a cross pattern if there are four.

Finish up. Replace the jack and tire iron in the trunk and store the hubcap there.

Be sure your teen understands that "donut" spares are not meant to be driven at highway speeds or over long distances. If your spare is a donut, it's imperative to drive to a service station and have the flat tire fixed or replaced as soon as possible.

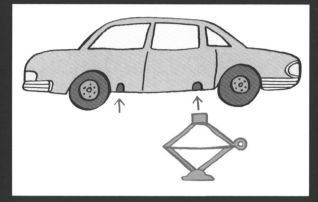

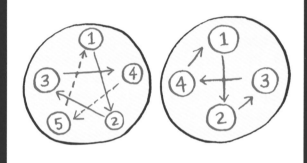

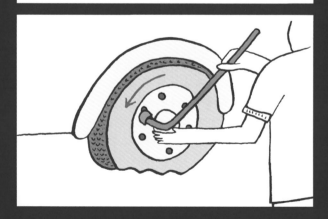

GUIDE YOUR TEEN TO THE RIGHT INTERNSHIP

You may be a titan of industry, but you know what it looks like from the bottom. You also know that no great career starts by accident; it's shepherded along a path that follows passion and potential. Help your teen find her path by getting her into an internship.

An internship is a chance for any young, bright-eyed go-getter to get a taste of what a given industry might be like to work in. Although many, if not most, internships are unpaid (or pay very poorly), the experience, invaluable contacts, and résumé gem are all fairly handsome rewards. Landing the right internship—one that will be in demand—means helping your teen have her ducks in a row.

Refine the presentation. Make sure your teen's résumé looks professional. Nobody expects her to have a lot of work experience, but there should be a fair amount of school achievement, rewards, and certainly some community service or volunteer experience. You can work with your future executive on crafting a killer cover letter that sells her initiative and value to the company. That letter is her chance to research the company and nail the interview with what she learns. She'll also need to clean up and dress well for the interview—and show up early.

Seek recommendations. Both you and your teen should network on social media and in person to see if anybody you know works in the industry where your youngster is targeting for an internship. Nothing lubricates the process like a glowing letter of recommendation.

Start early and apply often. In-demand internships at industry-leading companies fill up quickly. Most will recruit in January for a summer internship program. Counsel your teen to consider the process much like applying to colleges: She'll have her top choice, but she should keep her options open by applying to other interesting internship programs. Even if she comes up empty on internships, there is a fallback. She can always take the initiative and ask to "shadow" someone she admires in a company she might one day want to work for. It's not as involved as interning and doesn't really go on a résumé, but it offers the chance to make essential contacts and ask pertinent questions to figure out if the industry is really for her.

GIFT YOUR TEEN BASIC COOKING SKILLS

You may not be a star chef, but you can certainly educate your teen on how to prepare basic sustenance with recipes that are tasty, nutritious, and fairly easy. The best way to learn is by doing. Cook with your teen. Coach him to take his time, start simple, and don't be frustrated by failures.

Food-handling safety. The most important lesson is how not to poison himself. Emphasize that he always check expiration dates. If he can't find a date and is not sure, throw it out. Advise him never to mix cooked and uncooked proteins and to wash anything that touches uncooked proteins with hot, sudsy water. This includes cutting boards, knives, and his hands. Also stress he should wash his hands before any food preparation.

Mise en place. This is the fancy French term for gathering all ingredients before you ever start cooking. It's one of the best habits you can impart to your teen. It ensures everything the recipe calls for will be included and guarantees he won't get halfway through only to find that he is short a key ingredient.

Knife skills. Show your chef how to handle kitchen tools correctly. Keep knives sharp and always cut away from the body and fingers. Whenever he is chopping something, he should curl his fingers to hold it in place so that the face of the blade abuts the knuckles.

TEACH YOUR TEEN TO CHANGE A CAR'S OIL

If you consider yourself a jack-of-all-trades but take your car to some pricey drive-by lube place for servicing, shame on you. Not only should you change your own oil, but you should teach your teen how. It's a matter of self-reliance and saving about half what a shop would charge you.

Start with the supplies. Buy the oil recommended by the manufacturer. Using a different oil weight can void a warranty, and the right engine oil is a small expense that can pay big dividends in engine longevity. He'll also need to buy an oil filter—it's smartest to wait until he's removed the filter and check it against the one he's given at the auto parts store to make sure they're the same. He'll also need a funnel.

Drain the old. Run the car for about three minutes to ensure the oil is thin enough to drain completely. Turn off the car and remove the oil fill cap. Slide under the engine (unless the drain plug and/or filter can be accessed from above) with your teen. Avoid the exhaust manifold, which may be hot. Slide a 2-gallon (8L) plastic basin under the drain plug and use a wrench to loosen the drain nut. Unscrew it entirely and remove it. While the oil drains, use a filter wrench to twist off the oil filter counterclockwise.

Ensure against leaks. Have your teen use a rag to thoroughly clean the drain plug threads and the mating surface where the oil filter snugs down to the engine block.

Replace the filter. Tell your teen to put a small amount of fresh oil on his finger and run the finger around the rubber seal of the new filter. Then he should carefully screw the filter back on the threaded post by hand until the filter seems tight. Tighten the filter an additional quarter turn by hand. (If the car uses a cartridge oil filter, follow the manufacturer's instructions for replacement.)

Fill and complete. Replace the drain plug and tighten half a turn with a wrench. Use the funnel to add oil; add ½ quart (473.2 ml) less than the specified capacity. Be sure the oil fill cap is tight and run the car for about three minutes. Then turn it off, and let it rest for a couple of minutes. Check the dipstick and add more oil as necessary. Discard the oil and filter according to local waste regulations.

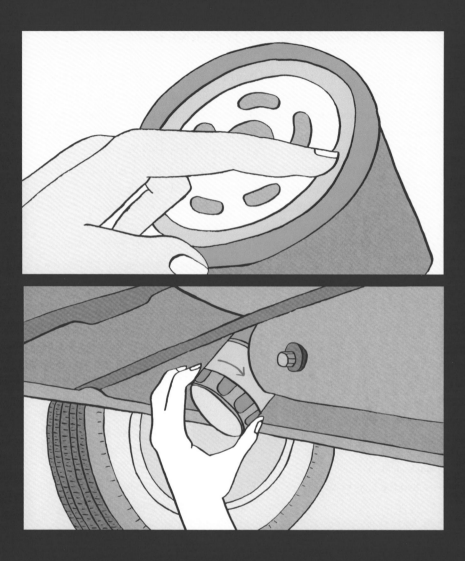

COACH A TEEN FOR A JOB INTERVIEW

It's never too early to prep your offspring for his future life, whatever that may be. Unless you have a budding entrepreneur on your hands, a big part of that future life is going to hinge on acing a job interview or two. Set him up for success on his very first job, and he's more likely to ultimately land the one that delivers the good life.

The first and most important lesson to impart about job interviews is to be prepared. That comes down to walking in looking like a winner, with an impressive presentation and answers to any question that might be asked.

Start with the résumé. This may be more filler than meat, but it should lay out a well-honed work ethic (something you can illustrate through even basic work like cutting lawns) and attention to detail (no misspellings or stains on the résumé). If your teenager really wants to knock the socks off a potential employer, he should come loaded with several personal references that can attest to the teen's reliability and maturity.

Show up with the answers. All employers want to know many of the same things: Will this person be reliable, a self-starter, and reflect well on the business? Those concerns lead the questions that will be asked at the interview, so help your teen develop succinct, hard-hitting and well-thought-out answers. Sit him down in a mock interview. Ask him, "Why do you want to work for us?" (The answer better be more than "To make money.") "Why would you be a good member of the team?" "Give an example of problem you've handled." Discuss the answers and talk about ways to make them stronger. The more you and your teen practice, the more at ease he will be during the actual interview.

Own the interview. Make sure your teen understands all the nonverbal cues that go into an interview. He should show up early and look sharp with combed hair, clean nails, and a teen's version of business casual. Go further as well and coach him to make direct eye contact, smile, and sit up straight—all important ways to make a great first impression.

PREP A TEEN TO DEAL WITH THE POLICE

You're a law-abiding dad. In the best of all possible worlds, your teen never has an interaction with a police officer. Why would he? You've taught him well, and you're a great role model. But all it takes is being in the wrong place at the wrong time and your kiddo can find himself speaking with authorities. A little advance planning might make the difference between a civil, brief interaction and something more serious.

The upside to having this talk with your teen is that the strategies you discuss will be useful for dealing with any authority figure, from someone behind the counter at the DMV to a grumpy professor in college. These are really lifelong tools. They can also be used to resolve conflicts in general.

Start with the end. Teach your teen that when approaching any possible conflict, it's wise to always ask yourself, "What outcome do I want?" and then work toward that. It can clarify a lot of communication.

Stay cool. It should go without saying that any police officer and most authority figures, for that matter, don't respond well to impatience, anger, or aggression. But say it to your teen. The calmer he can stay, the more he controls the situation.

Keep hands out. For understandable reasons, police officers always want to see a person's hands. Coach your teen to remove them from his pockets or, if in a car, immediately put them on the steering wheel and leave them there. And he should never talk to a cop with hand gestures—use words and keep still.

Fess up. If the unthinkable has happened and your teen has been doing something wrong—a beer or two with a friend, for instance—advise him to own up to it immediately under questioning. Things only go downhill by lying to police.

Be respectful. The word "sir" carries a lot of power and should be a big part of your teen's vocabulary if he ever interacts with the police. A bit of respect can become a two-way street and make the whole situation much more benign.

Communicate clearly. Make eye contact, speak clearly, and get to the point. Answer questions as directly as possible.

BE A POSITIVE ROLE MODEL

The enlightened dad knows that kids are always watching and can detect baloney a mile away. You are forever serving as an example for your kids, whether you're being good or bad. Where kiddos are concerned, it is definitely monkey see, monkey do. It's no coincidence that kids raised by parents who smoke, use drugs, or engage in domestic abuse are statistically much more likely to engage in those behaviors themselves. Modeling the best sort of good behavior is just a matter of mindful living. All you have to do is the right thing.

Control emotions. If you're quick to anger, change—for your own health and the mental health of your teen. Not only will she be reluctant to open up to a parent who might fly off the handle, she'll also learn from you that it is okay to fly off the handle in response to frustrating situations. Better to be boring, calm, and predictable.

Listen (even when you want to yell). Rather than jumping to a conclusion and jumping on your teen, gather all the facts about any incident and then come up with a reasonable conclusion. Even if that conclusion is punishment for your teen, she'll learn that hearing all the evidence is the best way to make a sound judgment.

Volunteer. Sure, it may seem like time you don't have, but you send a noble, lasting message of service to others and compassionate giving when you volunteer. Depending on the organization, you may even rope your teen into volunteering with you. The best type of quality time!

Model ideal behaviors. You certainly don't want to get drunk in front of your teen, smoke, or use drugs. But that's kind of a low bar. Obey traffic laws, pay your taxes on time, and do the usual drill for responsible citizens and you send a more subtle but no less important message that socially accepted behavior is the way to go.

Follow your own rules. The old parental saw, "Do as I say, not as I do," should not be your motto. You need to show your teen that there is no double standard and that you can follow the rules, even if you're the one that makes them.

POINT YOUR TEEN TOWARD MENTORING

Look at you, dad of the year, you raised yourself a responsible, caring human teen. You showed him how socially conscious, decent people conduct themselves, and he's following your lead. Now it's time for him to pass on those lessons.

Mentoring is a challenge that helps any teen mature. It's a way to help less fortunate kids. And, as a bonus, mentoring a youngster looks great on a college application. The real reward is less tangible. Mentoring can profoundly change a child's life; the personal reward for doing that is incalculable.

There is usually no special skill required. Your teen just needs to commit to a schedule so that his young charge can rely on him. It's just a matter of spending time playing catch, miniature golfing, or lending a sympathetic ear. If your teen is especially good at a school subject, he can tutor a younger child as part of mentoring.

Your teen can find mentoring opportunities through the YMCA, local elementary schools, local social services departments, summer camps, and traditional "peer mentoring" nonprofits found online. He can also establish a less formal mentoring relationship through friends of friends or family.

KICK AN OLLIE WITH YOUR TEEN

Few things are quite as satisfying as the look on a teen's face when he sees his dad pull off something completely unexpected—and that he would take pride in doing. The perfect example is performing an ollie on a skateboard. You'll need to practice this for a while before you can pull it off casually. But once you get the move, it will be second nature. It should go without saying that you need to wear proper safety gear whenever you're on a skateboard—a helmet, elbow guards, wrist guards, and possibly even knee guards can save you a lot of pain and embarrassment.

Break the move down into its three basic steps. You can practice each by itself. Also keep in mind, that if you wind up on your butt more than you'd like, you can practice the move with the trucks (the skateboard's wheels and axles) removed. When practicing an ollie, the steps will be easier to master if you're holding on to a low fence, handrail, or some other sturdy waist-high support.

❶ **Tip the nose.** Slide your back foot so it's right over the tail of the board, with your heel hanging off. Step on the tail to raise the nose. The tail should hit the ground.

❷ **Slide the front foot.** As the nose comes up, bend your ankle so that the sole of the front foot is at a right angle to the rear foot. Slide it lightly up the board to a few inches (cm) from the front.

❸ **Combine fluidly.** Bend your knees and coil yourself to jump. In one fluid motion, pop the tail down while you jump and slide your front foot forward to the nose. Lift your back foot up at the same time as the front, allowing the board to pop up off the ground. Stick your landing, bringing the front foot down in the middle of the board and the back foot in about 6 inches (15.2 cm) from the back of the board.

Once you're comfortable pulling an ollie, you'll be able to do other tricks to impress your teen, like riding a rail, an ollie flip, and more. Just let him have his own time at the skate park.

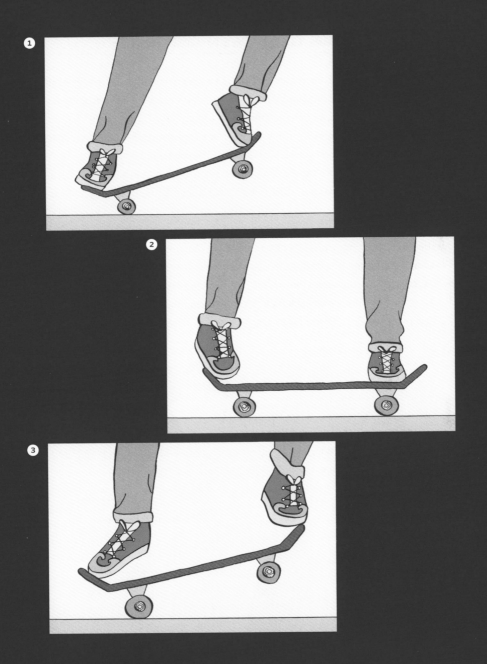

HELP YOUR TEEN DYE HAIR

Whether you have a girl or a boy, your teen may suddenly decide that colored hair is the fashion accessory du jour. What to do? If you really want to bond, give your teen the go-ahead . . . with qualifications.

Insist on temp. Temporary hair dyes abound; many are vegan and meant specifically for teens and tweens. These are easy to use and wash out after a brief time. Avoid adult hair dye, which is often specified for users no younger than 16.

Chalk it up. Hair chalk is a rather messy, easy-to-use, and temporary option. Have your teen apply it outside or in a garage to limit clean-up.

Start modest. Unless your teen is adamant about a head full of blue hair, limit the dye job to a smaller amount of hair as a trial.

Check the rules. School dress codes may prohibit dyed hair, and the look may not be appropriate for your teen's job. A little advance investigation can save a lot of hassle.

Keep away from roots. Make sure the dye never comes close to the roots or scalp; the hair should be dyed strand by strand.

BURY A TIME CAPSULE

This family activity is sure to capture the imagination of even a jaded teen, because teens have lived long enough to understand the value of memories.

You'll need a 5-gallon (19L) bucket with lid. It can be a used bucket as long as it's reasonably clean inside and the lid fits snugly. You'll also need a place to bury the capsule—either property you own and will for the foreseeable future or in your backyard if there is room and you feel like you'll stay in the house at least until retirement.

Now tell everyone in the family to pick two or three contributions (they have to fit in the bucket) that represent the current moment or recent past to them. The keepsakes can be photos, trophies, or anything else that each member of the family is willing to part with. Everyone also has to write a letter or postcard summing up what the world they inhabit is like.

Dig a hole about 4 feet deep by 2 feet wide (121.9 × 61 cm). Host a fun ceremony and mark the bucket with indelible ink or paint, noting date and family contributing to the capsule, before burying it for posterity.

PLAN A BONDING FAMILY VACATION

You're a smooth operator and someone who knows how to bring people together like a game-show host. You throw great parties, you make for special birthday celebrations, and now you face your most intriguing entertainment challenge: inspiring the whole family to join in planning the perfect, entirely memorable (for all the right reasons) family vacation.

The intense exposure to one another is what makes a family vacation the perfect bonding opportunity (and potential battle zone). Your teen has no doubt been working hard on his independence and forging his own life, but that doesn't mean you have to be disconnected. Organize an intriguing vacation and you celebrate a home-life relationship that will soon be changing radically as your teen heads off to college or other adventure (hopefully not your basement!).

The trick is to ensure the vacation has something for everyone. The beach person should get a chance to squeeze the sand between her toes, and the mountain guy should get the chance to go for a nice, bracing hike. The way to combine all that? A good old-fashioned road trip.

Have every member of the family (don't forget Dad!) pick two destinations. They have to be close enough to realistically tackle in the time allowed for the vacation, and everybody's choice should be in the same direction of travel from your location. The best way to achieve those things is to get out a paper map and use the computer to sift through possible destinations. Then plot the most efficient route to every-body's chosen attractions on the map. The planning itself can be a fun and engaging exercise and can build excitement for the trip.

Lodgings can be built into the destinations (a tent or just sleeping bags), or you can add to the adventure by picking out vacation rentals along the way—chosen by committee. Plan on taking plenty of pictures and possibly even keeping a digital journal of the trip, because you'll want to remember the epic adventure for a long time to come.

START A FAMILY NOVEL

Perhaps you've always wanted to unleash your inner Hemingway? Well, a book that the whole family contributes to is your chance. Group-written books are rarely literary masterpieces. What they are, though, is absolute fun and shared laughter.

Set up the project with a pen and notebook or go digital by creating a shared file online. Start the ball rolling by writing the first couple of pages, introducing major characters (suspiciously named for family members), and laying out the plot line. Will it be a murder mystery? A great sailing adventure? A crime thriller? All of the above?

Anything goes. The only rule is everybody contributes. It's naturally inspiring to tag onto a piece of writing that already exists, and family members can do it at their leisure so that it never becomes a burden. You'll be amazed at what a fantastic keepsake and conversation generator the ever-growing volume becomes.

INTEGRATE YOUR TEEN'S FRIENDS

Want your kiddo to hang around the house a little more? Invite him to bring his friends around and create a welcoming teen-friendly space.

Accept them. Drop any judgment you might bring to the table about your teen's friends. If you've raised him right, he's chosen good people for his inner circle. And, no matter what, some teens will always be a little annoying. It's the nature of the beast— and remember back to when you were a teen . . ..

Feed the mob. Want to win their hearts? Go through the stomach. But think bagel pizzas, not salad. Some junk food and sports drinks can make your kitchen the teen place to be. On the same note, occasionally invite a couple of his teen friends to stay for dinner. Few things are as effective at integrating friends than sharing a family meal with them.

Accept trade-offs. Yeah, you might lose access to your family room just when you were hoping to binge-watch your favorite TV series, but you'll be gaining access to your teen and know where he is and what he's doing.

Be friendly. Teen friends may become your kiddo's lifelong friends. Get to know them without prying. Ask open-ended, friendly questions that don't sound like grilling.

MAKE YOUR OWN OUTDOOR ADVENTURE EXPERIENCE

Wilderness adventure trips can be amazing, once-in-a-lifetime events. They provide teens with a whole new perspective on nature and our need to preserve it. It's also your chance to show your teen a different side of the at-home dad. Use any hiking and camping trip to teach your teen skills that will be useful for the rest of his life.

You don't have to go deep in the wilds for a month to get a full measure of character-building outside time. A trip to the nearest state wilderness preserve, national park, or even a larger forested area can fill the bill. And a long weekend is plenty of time for a deep dive into nature.

Keep it real. Car camping or living out of an RV, is all well and good. But those experiences limit exposure to nature. Sometimes being a little uncomfortable is part of growth. That's why you'll bring what you can carry—no refrigerated snacks, no oversized coolers, and no cozy bunks to sleep in.

Prep with the teen. Set up backpacks with your young camper. That includes dried food, emergency first-aid supplies, a basic camping kit (metal cup, fire-lighting device, toilet paper), and a bedroll, sleeping bag, or lightweight tent if you prefer.

Leave electronics behind. This will be the hardest mandate to enforce but is key to getting the most out of the trip.

Don't force activities. Maybe you're up for a 20-mile (32.2 km) hike over rocky terrain, but that doesn't mean your teen should be game. Be reasonable. The object is not to push you or your kid to the edge; it's to learn about and enjoy the wilderness. On the same note, you don't have to fill the time with after-dinner sing-alongs and bird-spotting competitions. A little dreamy stargazing may be more than enough for a memorable experience.

Teach skills. Skill building is a key feature of any wilderness adventure with a teen. Among the useful practices he should learn are how to gather kindling and wood and light a fire, the proper way to set up and break down a campsite, where and how to go to the bathroom, and ways to avoid insect bites, animal attacks, and injuries.

MAKE A MAGICAL MIX TAPE

There is magic in a mix tape. It's a way to show you care enough to spend time thinking about a person's taste and what she may like. A mix tape is a great birthday present for your teen or a celebratory surprise gift when she gets her license—she can listen to it on her first solo drives.

Make it digital. Mix tapes were originally custom-made cassettes or CDs. The modern version is a flash drive. It can be plugged into a computer and the files transferred to a phone or music player. You can buy packages that look like a cassette with a flash drive embedded in it, a great option for a gifted mix tape.

Theme it. Add interest with songs that share a common element, either the focus of the song or a particular word or phrase.

Pick a combo. Go a little bit wild by interspersing different genres and time periods. Choose at least ten songs so that your teen can skip any that she finds particularly grating and still have something to listen to.

KEEP YOUR TEEN TALKING

You're not Mr. Nosy, but you do want to head off problems like diving grades, broken hearts, and other teen calamities. Follow some basic communication guidelines, and you'll always be in the know.

Stay even keeled. If you want to keep your teen talking, suspend judgment and keep a tight lid on what might be your natural reactions to something he might say. Be careful never to make things a bigger deal than they need to be.

Listen. Getting a teen talking is about allowing room for words. That means listening and even sometimes allowing for silence. Listening is a hard skill to master, but it will make your teen feel that he is being heard and taken seriously.

Sit with it. You don't have to solve every problem, and your teen isn't necessarily asking you to. Often what he needs most is a sounding board to find his way to his own solution.

Give thoughtful feedback. When you do comment or respond in a conversation with your teen, be constructive. Always ask yourself this: "How does what I'm saying help?" It's important to be honest but diplomatic.

CONVINCE YOUR TEEN TO VOLUNTEER

Convincing a teenager to volunteer has all kinds of upsides. A challenging volunteer assignment, or a variety of them, simply looks fantastic on a résumé or college application.

More important, helping those in need and seeing how the less fortunate live, as well as dealing with a new world, is an unequaled perspective-expanding experience. That experience will build any teen's empathy. Being part of something wholly beneficial and positive is rewarding in its own right, a feeling that can't be replicated in a paying job. But speaking of paying jobs, volunteering is also an excellent way to network with like-minded people and may even lead to a paid position with the nonprofit.

Pitching those benefits is the first step toward getting your teen interested. There are other ways you can foster a desire to sign up. Keep in mind that the more excitement and energy you bring to getting him involved, the more likely your teen is going to engage with potential volunteering opportunities.

Play to his interests. You're most likely to get your teen on board if you suggest an opportunity that plays to his natural interests, hobbies, or passions. If he's an animal lover, volunteering at a shelter or animal-rescue organization is a good fit. A teen that has younger siblings and gets along well with them may respond to opportunities at a nonprofit preschool or after-school program.

Make it easy. You would hope that your teen takes the initiative, but sometimes desire is ahead of organization or follow-through. Do your teen volunteer candidate a solid, and gather all the specifics about volunteering for a given organization. Some need only a simple application; others may require a background check.

Be realistic. If the organization hits the sweet spot of his interests, your teen may be extremely excited to jump in. Unfortunately it's easy to overcommit. Keep your teen grounded when he's considering volunteering schedules; he needs to be sure to make time for sports obligations, a job if he has one, homework and class assignments, and a little personal downtime as well.

OWN THE GO-KART TRACK

Welcome to Funtown. Population: you and your teen. Want to rock your kiddo's perception of you and treat him to unrivaled fun? It's time for a trip to the go-kart track.

This is your chance to impress your youngster. Remember to outfit yourself with a helmet—usually mandated at legitimate go-kart establishments. Safety first, mega-fun second.

Lean back. To start with, you want to maintain maximum control of the kart. Press back into the seat at all times to maintain finesse on the brake and gas and have the ultimate responsiveness in the steering.

Drift. The coolest move you can show off is a drift. Approach from the outermost lane and take the turn at speed, feathering the brake. Turn into the inside lane. If you're turning left, lean back toward the right. Release the brake and keep the front wheels pointed in the track direction as the back wheels break free and drift. Accelerate evenly out of the drift, leaning into the curve, keeping the front wheels pointed straight along the track. The back wheels will come in line.

VISIT COLLEGES WITH YOUR TEEN

Buck up, Dad; you're not on a farewell tour. College visits are about a stage of life, and your kiddo is sure to be back to see you on a regular basis. (The more nerve-racking reality is all the money you're about to spend.)

College visits are a bonding opportunity and way to accompany your teen on the start of one of his most exciting life adventures. Here's how you can keep from screwing it up.

Read the teen. Know when there is no interest there. You may like the place, but if he doesn't, cross it off the list.

Don't tour impossibles. If your teen's grades and family particulars disqualify him from much financial assistance and the school is way out of your budget range, don't set your teen up for disappointment. Figure that out before you travel.

Take notes. You or the kiddo should be jotting down perceptions about each college. They can start to blur together, and it's nice to have something to refer back to. Focus on the things that will matter most to your teen and anything he specifically comments on.

Remember silence is golden. This is all about the kiddo. Assume he'll ask the questions he wants to ask. You can always call admissions later if you have questions of your own. Give him the reins of the visit and let him take the lead in coordinating the itinerary.

Enjoy overnight stays. This is a chance for the real bonding to begin, because hotels can be fun and a dinner out can be perfect for unwinding away from what will be a momentous decision for you both. Keep it light and breezy for the moment.

Check out what's key. Have a science nerd on your hands? Make sure the tour runs by the labs and science building or make an appointment to visit those yourselves. Get the lowdown on the lodging situation if it looks like your student-to-be will be staying in a dorm.

Stray beyond campus. What is the outside community like? Chances are your teen is going to want to venture out off campus—to go to parties or just pick up some clothes at the local mall. It's worth checking out what's close by.

Start a new hobby, get out there and meet new friends, or just goof off a little.

CHAPTER 6

Empty Nesting (or Not)

Ah, you old softy, you. You won't admit it, but you're a little bummed that the kiddo—or maybe the last of the kiddos?—packed up and moved out to the greener pastures of a dorm or an apartment with friends. It seems kinda quiet as you roam the old castle. There's nobody around to ask you, "What's for dinner?" or to be slamming doors without thinking. No extra dirty dishes in the sink or socks and underwear on the guest bathroom floor.

Well, no more moping, mister. This is a transition period, and like all transition periods, you're leaving something behind—but you're also heading into something exciting, something full of potential. That new thing is the chance to reclaim your house and turn it into the home of your dreams. It's also time to explore new opportunities and reconnect with your partner.

Throwing yourself and your significant other into redecorating or entertaining can be an excellent way to ease into the transition. You and your partner can put your stamp back on the interior that you call home and show off your unique style and taste. This type of creative freedom can be exhilarating. It's a little bit like recapturing a piece of a younger, more energetic, more carefree self. So that transition is starting to sound a little bit better now, isn't it?

This moment in time is also your opportunity to expand your life in fun new ways. More free time for those interests you never seemed to have the time to pursue, things that just seemed crazy for a guy with kids. Start a new hobby, get out there and meet new friends, or just goof off a little without coming back to your huge to-do list. On the flip side, this phase also gives you a little bit of time, space, and quiet to contemplate the next big change looming on the far horizon: retirement.

Of course, the best-laid plans of mice and men are subject to being upended by kids who return home. If they need a place to park between a college dorm and their own domicile, that's okay. You're ready, and this chapter will help. You can set the terms for a new and different relationship than you've ever had with your offspring. It can be your chance to have different kinds of fun with adult children—and eventually, their offspring!

MAKE A MEMORY BOX OR SCRAPBOOK

Even a tough-guy dad likes to take a stroll down memory lane every once in a while. With the kiddo gone, pictures, school art projects, and little league trophies may be your only connection to him for a while. Make the most of them by organizing them in one easy-to-find place.

If family history is captured mostly in photos, you can make a digital or physical scrapbook. Flipping through a book can be satisfying, but a slideshow program allows you to organize images and distribute the slideshow as a unit to anyone who wants to see—without any worries that it could be destroyed or lost in transit.

More than likely, you're a memory-box man. Are you a woodworker? If so, get yourself out to your shop and start crafting a memory box out of cedar or other tough, long-lasting wood. Judge the physical items you want to store and make it slightly larger than you need. Make a hinged cover and—voilà!—a trip down memory lane just waiting for you any time you want it.

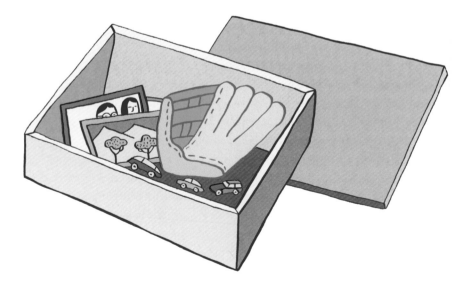

HOST A NOSTALGIA POKER GAME

Want to bring the college student home for something more than doing his laundry? It's time to put together an Ocean's Eleven–level poker game. A legitimate poker game is a perfect way to mark your evolving relationship with your child as he becomes more of an equal and less of a charge under your control.

The right poker game calls for a real, green felt table (or tabletop) and at least five players. Get yourself a set of real ceramic poker chips to re-create the feel of a casino game. The trappings are everything when it comes to making a poker game memorable. You'll also need the traditional poker spread: chips and dip, cold cuts and rolls, condiments, and a selection of beverages including adult and not.

Invite five to six players for a game that moves at a good pace but is still social. Plan on playing basic games like five- or seven-card stud and five-card draw. That ensures you don't leave anyone in the weeds or create frustration. Keep the stakes low for a friendly game.

ACING THE DRAMA-FREE HOLIDAY

You don't have to be Santa Claus dad to bring joy and gifts into your family's life during a holiday celebration. A stress- and conflict-free get-together isn't about perfection; it's about laughing, bonding, fun, and—most of all—creating cherished memories for everyone in attendance.

If you haven't seen your kid or kids (not to mention your grandkids—yoiks!) for some time, there can be a pressure to be the perfect host and make every moment just like a greeting card commercial. That way lies disappointment. The key is actually to relax and enjoy the moment, and your guests will, too.

Plan ahead . . . but don't overplan. If you or your significant other are fussing over a million and one details, you'll likely be far too stressed to relax yourself, much less create a pleasant atmosphere for everyone else. Didn't buy the right beer or remember to get those chips everyone loves? So what? The most important things to include in any holiday celebration are the people.

Pick fun indoor activities. Many holidays come around during bad-weather months. Being cooped up with a lot of other people can naturally fray nerves. A board game, a treasure hunt, "chill time," or a between-meals meal can loosen up the gathering and relax everyone.

Keep conversation light. All depending on how large your family is and how many people you've included in your family gathering, there may be a range of political opinions, religious beliefs, and general temperaments represented. That's a recipe for clashing wills and arguments. Head off any problems by leading mealtime conversations to positive places: favorite memories of holidays past, best gifts received, and vacation plans.

Absence creates fondness. Holidays can involve a lot of bad-for-you food and sedentary activities. It makes sense to invite some or all of your guests on brief excursions out of the house, whether it's a long walk, a little brisk throwing of the football out back, or even a half-day trip to a local landmark.

Set the score. Music can have a remarkable effect on mood and memory. That's why you should consider adding an upbeat soundtrack to your holiday celebration. Make a mix for the occasion, with some odd choices from your kid's youth.

PUT ON THE PERFECT FAMILY COOKOUT

Who can resist the allure of perfectly prepared hamburgers, steaks, and chicken; grilled corn on the cob; and all the trimmings? If you're the type of dad who hosted cookouts as a regular occasion, your kiddo has fond memories of summer days spent enjoying the backyard and devouring a flame-kissed feast. Time to gather the tribe by firing up the grill again, as only you can.

Draft the guest list. This is one family occasion where the more, the merrier. You may have grandchildren in the mix, returning friends from your child's youth, neighbors your kiddo knows well and likes, and family friends. Remember older, less mobile members of the family as well. A nice-weather gathering is a chance for your adult offspring to reconnect with his grandma or older relatives. The right cookout offers something for everyone, so there is nobody who won't feel at home.

Feed the beasts. Cookouts are all about delicious summer food. Make sure you grill an assortment of proteins as well as something for the few vegetarians that are sure to show up. Grilling food normally prepared in other ways, such as corn on the cob or potatoes is a great way to add to the cookout. Don't skimp on sides with traditional potato and macaroni salads, baked beans, and other family favorites. Beverages are part of the picture, and it's a good host's obligation to provide alcoholic and nonalcoholic options. And do not leave out the dessert. A good refrigerator cake or a few fruit pies are the cherry on the sundae of a good cookout. And remember: better too much food than too little.

Bring out the games. There's no crime against guests just chilling out and enjoying the spread and good company, but a few outdoor games can add another element to any cookout. Beanbag toss is a classic that is ideal for kids, friends, and even small grandkids. Horseshoes is another time-tested cookout game, and bocce ball is engaging and entertaining to watch and can include players of all ages.

Take the music with you. Wireless-enabled speakers were just about invented for cookouts. You'll need a playlist that includes favorites that everyone will recognize and like. Avoid extreme genres or songs—or sleepy stuff. (Death metal and piano bar classics are both a no.)

GAMING WITH GRANDKIDS

Sure, you consider yourself a contemporary man who keeps up with the times, right? Well, wake up, Grandpa; at few points in history have the cultural and social differences between generations been more pronounced than the current moment. But no worries, man; you can bridge that divide with the power of video games.

The beauty is, this is a way to connect with your grandkid whether you're both in your living room or a thousand miles apart. Thank goodness for online games.

You can play on your computer or on a streaming device connected to your TV. In either case, the faster the processor is, the better your—and your grandkiddo's—experience will be. Using a game console with your TV offers the benefit of a fairly understandable controller for any game; but the computer keyboard and mouse will be more precise in certain techniques in any game, especially shooting faraway opponents.

Film it. Another reason for using a computer is that most have built-in cameras, while many TVs do not. A camera will allow you and your grandkid to see each other's faces and reactions in in-game video feeds. Of course, that's important only if you're playing at a remove. If you're side by side, you'll need an extra controller or two computers.

Get a headset. A big part of the fun of gaming together is chatting while you're doing it. Inexpensive earbuds with a microphone won't set you back much, but they also won't provide very good sound. Make a quantum leap in quality by spending a little more money on a bottom-of-the-range gaming headset.

Up your game. If you suck at whatever game you two play, it's not going to be particularly fun for either one of you. That's because, in most games, you'll be playing as your grandkid's partner and your bad play will make both of you less competitive. Practice a little.

Schedule play. Don't assume you can just luck into finding your grandkid playing on any given evening and jump right in. Even if you happen to log in to a game while your grandchild is playing, he might be competing with or against friends and won't necessarily appreciate sharing the airtime with Grandpa. Always arrange sessions in advance.

FILM LIFE LESSONS AND LAUGHERS

You might not be an award-winning director, but, man, that camera you have in your phone can make you at least a rookie filmmaker. (Of course, if you have an old or inexpensive cell phone, your filming options may be limited. In which case, a digital video recorder is your next purchase.)

A basic digital video editor will make all the difference. The key to making keepsake videos that will connect you with kid and grandkid is to film way more than you need and then edit it down to something short and profound or funny.

Although you should have long ago gotten in the habit of regularly filming family moments and developmental stages in your child's (now grandchild's) life, you should be more purposeful in what you film.

Write a script. It may sound odd but take a minute and jot down what type of video you want to make and a bare-bones outline of what will be in it. It's not a Hollywood production, but you should have an idea of the goal before you spend time filming.

Be thoughtful or funny. This is a wonderful way to leave "life lessons" or just a legacy for grandchildren. But it's also an incredible tool for showing your humorous side and amusing your heirs. You might be surprised after you make one video that you have a knack for serious or humorous.

Overfilm. It's digital. All it costs you is a little time recharging the phone's batteries. So shoot way more video than you need and you might be surprised at the gems you find in editing.

Enjoy editing. Simple video editors (some computers and computer operating systems come equipped with native video-editing programs) are fairly easy to use. Once you master the basics, you can explore special sounds and effects. Use it to explore your creativity and have fun with it.

Limit distribution. If this is for your family, be careful where you upload. Once you put a video on social media—even on your own page or account, and even if it's set to "private"—that video can be picked and used by others in ways you might not appreciate.

REDESIGN AN EMPTY KID'S ROOM

You don't have start subscribing to an interior design magazine to capably redesign an unused kid's bedroom into something more accommodating of your current life stage. Yes it was thoughtfully parental to keep the space as it was so that your returning college student could feel comfortable and welcomed. But now that your offspring is totally independent and you are truly an empty nester, it's time to update that nest.

Although you have a lot of options when it comes to repurposing an old kid's bedroom, one of the best updates for the space is turning it into a guest bedroom. The process is basic and doesn't require specialized skills. Take your time with it and it will be a long time before you want to change it.

The sketch. You can do this digitally or by hand (a pencil sketch is easier for most people to edit). Measure the room's dimensions and transfer them—on a scale of 1 foot (30.5 cm) to ½ inch (1.8 cm)—to a sketchpad or blank sheet of paper. Include door swing, window, and electrical outlet locations. Position the furniture for the room. You can sketch this into the floor plan or make the process easier by cutting out shapes to match the furniture you want to use and then playing around with the positioning until you're happy with it.

The colors. After you know where everything will go, pick the room's color scheme. Use paint chips to choose two or three colors that will dominate the room, along with perhaps a stronger or bolder accent color. Then buy tester jars of the paint colors and paint square-foot swatches in the room to judge how the colors look in natural light.

The textiles. Softer elements like curtains, bedspreads, and throw pillows add texture and variation in the room, as well as introducing splashes of color. Make sure the textiles serve their utilitarian purpose in addition to looking nice—curtains blocking morning light, for instance.

The finishing touches. Add any additional lighting, such as bedside reading lamps, to fill out the lighting in the room. Choose wall art and decorative accessories like vases that will reinforce the color scheme you've chosen. Add a rug to make the floor more comfortable underfoot as needed.

DECLUTTER LIKE A MONK

An upside to not having your kiddo around is that your empty nest can be clean and spare. A clutter-free space is calmer and more pleasant. Now's your chance to have that Zen house you've always dreamed of.

Weed out. The first step to a clutterless house is to remove what doesn't matter. Set aside boxes for donations or the dump and cast a critical eye on the other possessions in each room. Books with information that can easily be found online? Gone. Old music star posters? Gone. Broken toys, broken lamps, cheesy wall art? All gone. Be decisive and brutal. If it doesn't help you enjoy your home or isn't functional, lose it.

Rethink and rearrange. Once you've cleared out, consider the role each room plays. Focus on that purpose and arrange the furniture to facilitate intuitive traffic flow and make the room as pleasing to the eye as possible.

Introduce new. You'll find some gaps in your décor. You may want a clock in the kitchen or a vase for fresh-cut flowers from the garden for your dining room. Thoughtfully and carefully add these accents.

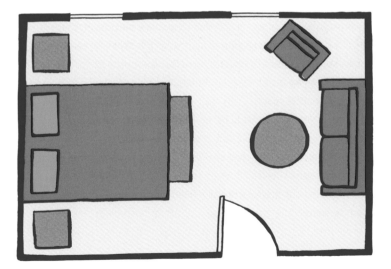

TURN THE EMPTY-NEST BEDROOM INTO A DREAM SPACE

Seize the opportunity, sir! You can have the room you've always thought you deserved in that newly empty home. Once your kiddo is out of the house (and it's clear that he's going to stay that way) you can remake his room into a refuge that captures the very best of your imagination.

Make a man (or woman) cave. Maybe you've always dreamed of a hideaway dedicated to indulgence, equipped with a refrigerated beer tap; a huge, plushy recliner; and a 60-inch plasma TV. You envision having the friends over for a game and spending some quality bonding time. Maybe you could never convert your garage because the pesky cars needed their space. Well exult. Now is your moment. Get out all those old sports trophies because now you have a place to display them. And don't forget the dartboard. Of course, it may be that your better half needs her own place to hide away with her gal pals. Be the gentleman and help her create a "she cave" where she can indulge her inner decadent woman.

Create a craft center or hobby room. Perhaps you're an avid fisherman who craves his own workshop for tying flies. Maybe it's model building. Or it could be that you are one of the last great stamp collectors. A stand-alone room offers you the chance to nurture any of these hobbies, giving them the space they deserve and keeping your precious particulars safely away from prying grandkids. Of course, you might be married to a painter, scrapbooker, or avid quilter (or maybe she's the one who needs a place to get her fishing gear in order). In that case, be a gracious spouse and set her up in her own dedicated space.

Check out a library. You don't have to call it a library. Really it's just a well-equipped reading room in your house, but library sounds so much more sophisticated. You'll need a very comfortable reading chair or chairs, a strong reading lamp, and a mess of books (with handsome shelves on which to put them). A library can be a wonderful refuge from the day's stress, especially when the weather is not conducive to daydreaming on the patio.

STORE WHAT THE KID LEFT BEHIND

You're a sensitive guy, but eventually it's time to take down all those markers of your kiddo's childhood. Store them and you leave open the option that your adult child can take a trip down memory lane when and if he chooses. The trick is storing things so that they don't take up too much of your valuable storage space and so that they are well organized for when you hand them off to your offspring.

Local storage. Smaller memorabilia is best stored in sturdy storage boxes with lids. Clearly mark what's inside and tape boxes shut (unless you're using plastic storage bins with lids that snap securely closed—always a good idea). The boxes should be small enough to easily fit in the available space in your garage, attic, or basement or in a closet. Wherever you store them, try to make sure they won't be exposed to moist conditions or vermin.

Rented storage. You may come across larger items such as memory-triggering furniture (your kid's favorite beanbag chair, for instance) that you're reluctant to donate or toss. If this is the case, it may be wiser to rent a small storage space. These spaces are secure, safe from the elements and the occasional disaster that may strike your home (water heater leakage), and won't eat up a huge amount of budget. It's a way to hold on to furnishings your kid may eventually want for your grandkids.

Reframe and repurpose. You don't necessarily have to hide away everything from your child's past. Some of those retro collectibles and ephemera can be repurposed as cool decorative accents. For instance, the thirty-year-old toy car collection can be organized by color in a shadow box to grace a country kitchen. Aged black-light posters can be framed and used as ironic art in your man cave.

The discard pile. Some stuff just isn't worth keeping. If you want to perform due diligence, send your kid a quick text and ask before you toss—but don't be surprised if he is less sentimental than you expected. The point is not to keep every last shred of evidence from your kiddo's youth. You only want to hold on to meaningful keepsakes.

HELP ADULT KIDS MANAGE FINANCES

You've been smart with your money. You've set yourself up for retirement and beyond, after a lot of hard work. You thought once you paid for college, you were done with the financial part of child rearing. But sometimes, accounting dad needs to come to the rescue. The number one financial problem for young people just starting out in their careers is credit spending. One card can lead to another, which can lead to a morass of debt. Reassure your child that there is a way out.

Budget. Start with your kiddo's budget (if she doesn't have one, start there). Diving into the details can be unpleasant but also revealing. Often just having an objective, detached third party run the figures can uncover problem areas. You'll likely identify obvious line items that can be reduced or cut entirely with a little discipline.

Stress focused saving. It is difficult for young people to set aside part of their income each month. That's even harder for something as ephemeral as a "rainy day fund." Instead help your adult child figure out savings goals, such as retirement, home buying, or other focal points that give savings a tangible element.

Discuss a financial advisor. Your child may feel she doesn't make enough to hire a financial advisor. But the whole point of a financial advisor is to help clients save more and put that money to work on its own. If your kid is resistant, make her a birthday or Christmas present of an initial consultation. That way, she can at least get a better idea of what an outside pro could do for her.

Loan; don't give. Worst-case scenario, your kid needs a short cash infusion to make it through a rough patch. If you decide to provide direct financial assistance, give it with strings very much attached. First and foremost, make it a loan rather than a gift. That will ensure that your child takes it as seriously as she should and doesn't look at you as an ATM to be used every time she's in trouble. The goal is to promote responsible behavior. To that end, set up rules for the loan. For instance, if she wants the money, she has to give up the five-dollar morning lattes.

ESTABLISH RULES FOR A BOOMERANG KID

It's a sad fact of our modern times that a great number of college graduates and even older kids have to return home to live for one reason or another. You're a stand-up dad, so you'll welcome your older kid home—with qualifications.

The key here is that a child returning to the home front is coming back to a much different relationship than the one she had when she left. She most likely won't process that, so you need to. A few simple rules will make clear that things are different and that expectations are much higher than they were when she was a child.

The conversation. Before she even starts to move her belongings home, you need to insist on a sit-down conversation to lay out limits and rules. This will be an uncomfortable talk but not as uncomfortable as when three years roll by and you still have a mopey twenty-something lounging in her bedroom while she pushes thirty. Be specific about what you expect in terms of behavior, and try to think about areas of conflict so that you can head off any problems before they happen. It's a wise move to take notes about what you discuss. That's a good way to make your kiddo know that you're serious and to keep her honest in the long run.

Fair share. She's your child, yes, but now she is also a roommate. It's hard to motivate yourself to progress if you're enjoying a free ride. That's why she's got to chip in for things like food and movie rentals. If she is really broke and truly can't afford a trip to the grocery store, she needs to put skin in the game instead. That means making meals a few times a week (not out of can or microwaved dinners) or handling chores you don't want to do. Those chores should be part of the deal anyway.

Balance of roles. You are going to have to walk the fine line between being a parent and being a landlord. Enforce the provisions that you laid when you first sat down to talk about the arrangement but shift gears if she really needs counseling and a sounding board through what can be a hard time in anyone's life.

TRANSITION TO A NEW FAMILY DYNAMIC

Part of a being an enlightened parent (and you are certainly the most enlightened of dads) is fluidly changing gears as your child changes life stages. You didn't talk to or treat a toddler the same as you would a teen, and the same goes for your adult child.

Now you have to shift gears once again. Don't fall back into old patterns; make an effort to allow your child to be the man (or woman) he wants to be. On the upside, you can let go of a lot of the requirements of parenting and embrace a new role as friend and advisor.

Give and get respect. Your evolving relationship with grown-up children is a transition to equality. You expect your kiddo to respect you in all ways, and you have to return the favor. Respect his time and his opinions. Be open to disagreements and debates; chances are he may know as much or more than you on certain subjects (well, at least allow the possibility).

Keep lines of communication open. Nobody's perfect, bub. You're going to stumble once in a while, and when you do, it will be essential that you have an open line of communication with your kiddo. You want him to feel he can come to you for advice or as a confidential sounding board who won't judge. Look closely and don't fall into old patterns of communication. When your child was young, father knew best and yours was the law of the house. Now you're talking with someone closer to a contemporary, and he governs his own life. In communicating with adult children, it pays to stress the adult part.

Maintain humor. As with all stages of child development, a light touch can be a saving grace. If you can laugh at your own foibles and gently poke fun at his, you foster the informal but effective give and take that makes everything easier. "Maintaining humor" also means letting go of anger. Exploding in anger at your adult child is unlikely to accomplish anything except for leaving bad feelings in your wake. Explode with laughter instead.

START A CLUB OR TEAM

The kiddo is gone, the house is quiet, and now it's "you" time. Expand your social life by putting together a club or team and you will make new friends and reconnect with old ones, have fun, and perhaps even get some exercise.

Sports. A team is a social bonding experience, but it's also a commitment. The bigger the team and the longer the season, the more intense the experience will be. Start small with a bowling team. It often requires only one night a week, and members can be recruited off the league's physical or digital bulletin board. Assemble a foursome for an annual charity golf tournament involves modest effort. Ready for something more ambitious? Manage a softball team or create a team for a local adult basketball or volleyball program.

Hobbies and passions. Forming around a shared passion is a natural. It can spur you to dive into a hobby you love but haven't had the time to pursue. Any avid interest can be shared: vintage cars or motorcycles, books, gardening (including specialized versions like orchid cultivation), model building, woodworking, hiking, or even beer making.

PLAN A BUCKET-LIST VACATION

Hallelujah! You and your partner's time is now officially your own. Most people hold off on bucket-list goals—those once-in-a-lifetime experiences that we dream of accomplishing—because there is never a right moment, enough money, or the will to jump in with both feet. But now is the perfect time.

Budget. Balance the goal to available budget. Some bucket-list pursuits will be far more expensive than others. You may also be able to combine more than one to optimize the money you spend—as in the case of two activities located geographically close together, incurring only one lodging fee.

Schedule. It's easy to be overly ambitious. But you'll sap a lot of the fun out of the adventure if you try to book too much into a short time frame. Sometimes one destination or activity done at a leisurely pace can be more rewarding than two that you rush through.

RECAPTURE YOUTHFUL ENTERTAINING

As an official empty nester, you now have the luxury of recapturing the pure enjoyment of being a host and throwing party.

The gang. For your adult evening, invite the most entertaining people in your circle but include a mix of personality types.

The setting. You can theme the party or go casual, but the baseline is a clean house and a few candles. Fresh-cut flowers? A nice, easy, classy touch. Do more than one vase.

The music. Music is mood, so consider your music carefully. It's good to play a mix or a series of albums, but the jams have to be lively enough to promote conversation and interaction, though not so bumping that people feel like they're in a club.

The food (and drink!). Even if it isn't a sit-down dinner, your party needs some high-end edibles. Pick them up a selection at the deli counter in an upscale market. Or if you're comfortable in the kitchen, throw together a diversity of finger snacks. Don't forget a selection of both adult and nonalcoholic beverages—and anyone who comes through the door should have some sort of drink in their hand inside of two minutes.

BE READY FOR THE NEXT STAGE

Man, oh man, retirement can sneak up on you. You thought you were all over it, didn't you? Planned the financial investments carefully. Watched your bottom line like a hawk. You figured out how much you had to invest to get to that magic finish line. You're ready to go out the door when that day comes. But you never sat down and thought, "What's next?"

Now's the time, brother. Don't waste another minute.

Budget out. If you planned correctly, you have enough money according to some actuarial formula to live your life comfortably until the end of it. But is that what it was all about? To spend day after day, comfortable, puttering around in the yard or your garage? Chances are you were smart enough to have additional investments beyond your retirement account. So what are you waiting for? Think about trips you always wanted to take and experiences you always hoped to have. Put some of your budget skills toward figuring out how to knock each one of those off the list. It may not be an all-at-once proposition, but you can certainly afford one adventure this year.

Choose fulfillment. Your adventures may not have anything to do with money. Maybe you had always dreamed of working in the nonprofit sector, something with early-childhood development, or housing the homeless. Well now's your chance to work for free.

Go (a little bit) wild. It's easy once you hit retirement to fall into the trap of thinking that new skills and learning are for the young. After all, haven't you done everything you needed to do? Well it's not about that; it's about making sure you don't become calcified. Did you once dream of learning to fly? Why not do it now that you have the chance to really immerse yourself? Nothing stopping you, buster. Or maybe the underwater world is calling to you. Get certified as a scuba diver. Learn a new language. Spend a long weekend in racing school. Learning should be a lifelong process, and now you get to do it just for fun!

MEDITATING FOR A NEW PERSPECTIVE

You and your significant other have more time than you know what to do with. You could start a new hobby or throw a party. But you could also institute a new healthy practice to keep you mentally supple and a little bit healthier into your golden years and beyond.

Now is the time to look to new horizons, and one of the best is meditation. Regular meditation can lower your blood pressure, increase your feeling of well-being, and improve your sleep. And all you need is twenty to thirty minutes a day. Meditation is, in short, the gift that you give yourself—one that keeps on giving. There are many different types of meditation, and you should select the one that speaks to you.

Transcendental meditation (TM). TM is popular around the globe as a practice that can calm, relax, and expand creativity in regular practitioners. It's a simple but incredibly useful practice to learn. The teacher gives you a mantra that is all your own. You sit with your eyes closed—in a chair, on a bench, on a cushion—and repeat the mantra silently, focusing on it and it alone. Most practitioners practice for about twenty minutes a session.

Guided meditation. As it sounds, this is meditation that follows prompts. You play a CD or digital file of a recording that usually includes both calming music and a person's voice guiding you through the meditation and telling you what to picture in your mind. The meditations tend to be built around systems such as chakras and are done with the eyes open or closed, although closed is usually the preference.

Tranquility meditation. This is the Buddhist practice of focusing on the breath or your own pulse and making an effort not to let the mind wander, dismissing any thoughts as they arise. Tranquility meditation is traditionally done sitting cross legged on a meditation cushion with the eyes open.

Focused meditation. This is a style of meditation that uses a prop—it can be a candle burning, a picture, a sound, or any other ongoing sensory experience. You concentrate on the focal point, screening out all other mental activity. This, too, is usually performed sitting on a meditation cushion with the eyes open.

COOK FOR TWO

You and your significant other are probably very used to cooking for a hungry, hungry youngster. It wasn't just your kiddo; inevitably a friend or two showed up. Nothing ever went to waste, and you didn't have to worry about scaling back. But the empty-nest kitchen is different. Not only will you be cooking for two now, but your appetites are probably more modest than a growing youngster's.

Make single-unit dishes. Turn to food that lends itself to individual units: sandwiches and panini; fajitas or burritos; and steaks, fish fillets, or chicken breasts. These will be much easier to control in terms of portion size.

Leverage your freezer. Got a good deal on bulk veggies or fruits in season? Exploit it by washing, drying, and then freezing them. They'll be good for smoothies, soups, stews, and other recipes. Your freezer is also your alternative to fussing with downsizing recipes. Make a normal batch of your favorite dish and freeze the extra.

Explore new resources. You'll find a wealth of cookbooks tailored to two-person serving sizes, and some recipe websites include tools for automatically cutting any recipe in half.

REINTRODUCE ROMANCE

You're suave. You're a smooth operator. You're just a little rusty after all those years. But romance rarely happens by accident. Make an effort and the reward will far outstrip your investment!

Plan for quality one-on-one time. What's the rush, sailor? It's time to get back to basics and woo the person you love. That means long walks, holding hands, and lots of communication. That's how you both started, and that's how you're going to restart.

Start dating. Chances are you've gotten out of the habit of actually going on dates. But that's the fun of romance. Imagine that you're going out for the first time. Where would you take her? What would knock her socks off? Yeah, do that. Try the unexpected and fun. Mini golf? Cooking classes? Go wild and get out of your comfort zone.

Be spontaneous. Romance is about spontaneity. Surprise her with flowers for no good reason. Treat her to Valentine's Day in October, with chocolates on the table and rose petals in the bedroom. Whisk her away for a long surprise weekend along a beach.

Index